Parenting Your Transgender Teen

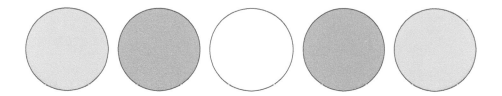

Positive Parenting Strategies for Raising Transgender, Nonbinary, and Gender Nonconforming Teens

Andrew Maxwell Triska, MSW, LCSW

ROCKRIDGE
PRESS

For general information on our other products and services or to obtain technical support, please contact our Customer Care Department within the United States at (866) 744-2665, or outside the United States at (510) 253-0500.

Rockridge Press publishes its books in a variety of electronic and print formats. Some content that appears in print may not be available in electronic books, and vice versa.

Interior and Cover Designer: Mando Daniel
Art Producer: Hannah Dickerson
Production Editor: Dylan Julian
Production Manager: Martin Worthington

All illustrations used under license from iStock.com and Shutterstock.com
Author photo courtesy of Samantha Barbaro

Paperback ISBN: 978-1-63878-883-6 | eBook ISBN: 978-1-63878-502-6
R0

Contents

Introduction

You probably picked up this book because your teenager just told you something important about themself. You want to be supportive, but what does *supportive* mean for trans teens? As a therapist who works with teens who are trans, nonbinary, gender nonconforming, and gender-questioning (as well as with their parents and caregivers), I've seen many families quickly go from confusion and anxiety to support and understanding when they began to learn more about gender identity and listen to their child's experiences. For you, that starts with curiosity about those experiences and the ability to allow your child to teach you about themself, just as you taught them about the world when they were smaller.

It's normal not to know much about the fine points of gender identity. These topics probably weren't covered in school or by your own parents during "the talk." In fact, gender and sexuality may not have been something your family felt comfortable talking about at all. And as an adult, you might have seen stories in the media that painted an inaccurate picture of what trans people's lives are really like. Even if you're trans yourself, or are part of the larger LGBTQ+ community, you may still have more questions than answers about your child's experiences, and it might be tough to separate your own feelings and experiences from those of your child.

Relationships with teens are tricky no matter what the circumstances. A growing brain means a need for more independence and choice. It's hard for some families to overcome the strangeness of seeing a teenager make decisions and solve problems on their own when they were helping the same kid cross the street just a few short years ago. It's tempting to jump in and say, "You don't know what you're doing yet—but I do, and I'll tell you!" It's equally tempting to say nothing because you don't know what to say or you're afraid you'll make things worse.

Parenting a trans teen means getting comfortable with risk and uncertainty. There will be many, many times when you say the wrong thing, or when nothing you say seems to be the right thing. Bullying and discrimination might make you want to protect your child, even at times when they tell you they need more freedom and autonomy. Letting go of the reins and allowing your teen to make decisions that seem big and life-altering may leave you feeling unmoored. There may even be times when no path forward seems 100 percent safe and comfortable. This book will give you the tools to manage your own anxieties around your teen's gender identity, and to parent in a way that respects your need to teach and guide your child—and your child's need for independence.

What Is Positive Parenting?

Positive parenting is a term used to describe parenting strategies that emphasize sensitivity to the child's needs and prioritize warmth and flexibility over power and control. Families who use these strategies choose to focus more on reinforcing their child's good qualities than punishing their bad behavior.

Positive parenting is also *mindful*. Positive parenting strategies make you ask questions like, "Why am I doing this? What outcome do I want? Am I doing this because it makes *me* feel better? What am I telling my child with my behavior?" These are especially crucial questions when you're parenting a trans teen. You're sure to have powerful emotions about what's going on in your child's life, and positive parenting will help you put these emotions into context and channel them in more helpful ways.

It's easy to read parenting blogs written by cheerful, rosy-cheeked families who sit together in pumpkin patches and think, "Why is everyone else's parenting so happy and effortless?" Don't get the impression that positive parenting means having no negative emotions about parenting, or never having moments when you want to tell your child exactly what you think of their friend Kyle. Positive parenting encourages you to recognize your emotions and reflect on where they're coming from rather than let them rule your behavior. It also provides the space for you to make mistakes—even big ones—and to take responsibility for them.

The good news is you're probably already using some positive parenting strategies. Psychologist Diana Baumrind divided parenting styles into three types: *authoritarian, permissive,* and *authoritative.* In this model, authoritarian parents demand perfection from their children without being responsive to their children's needs, focusing on their own need for control and order at the expense of their children's need for understanding and flexibility. Permissive parents, on the other hand, offer only loose boundaries and limits, and prioritize their children's happiness and comfort over their children's responsibilities toward others. Contrasting these two are authoritative parents, who strike a balance. Authoritative parents give their children boundaries and hold them accountable but are also empathetic, allowing their children to make decisions for themselves—and to make mistakes and learn from them.

In this book, I'll recommend positive parenting strategies to help you strike that balance. Good news: If you've ever withheld judgment about your teen's decision to buy a Nintendo Switch instead of saving their money or trusted them to drive their friends to a movie for the first time without tagging along to make sure they didn't run any red lights, you've already used positive parenting skills.

It's important to remember that positive parenting emphasizes boundaries: clear distinctions between where your responsibilities end and your teen's control over their own life begins. Families without boundaries are sometimes called *enmeshed*. In these families, teens often struggle to separate their identities from those of their parents, and parents sometimes feel that their child's autonomy and individuation is a threat to the family.

This pattern can cause teens to become too dependent on their parents, or to keep secrets to avoid their parents' disapproval. Positive parenting can interrupt that cycle and help parents and teens get more comfortable with the idea that difference and disagreement are fully compatible with—and necessary to—love and closeness.

How to Use This Book

This book is organized into five chapters. The first covers a brief history of trans identities and how gender has been categorized and studied. We'll spend some time talking about the way culture has shaped the way we talk about gender, bodies, and identity. We'll also look at scientific research on gender identity that might help you put your child's gender identity into context.

In the second chapter, we'll talk about the terms used to describe gender identity and provide you with language that will offer you more accurate and affirming ways of talking to your teen about their experiences.

In chapter 3, we'll look at the ways you can support your teen around their gender expression, like finding clothes that fit or going to a gender-affirming salon. We'll also discuss why gender expression is so important in the first place. In chapter 4, we'll talk about some of the changes your teen might want to make to their body (now or in the future) and other body needs like inclusive sex education.

In the final chapter, we'll look at ways you can create a supportive home environment for your teen and advocate for them in the larger world. You'll learn about how to talk about your teen's gender to friends and family, how to support your child in school, and the laws that protect trans people from discrimination and harassment.

Each chapter contains sidebars with answers to questions that might have come up for you when your child told you about their identity but that you'd rather not have to ask your child. You'll also find a parenting tips section at the end of each chapter that offers strategies to help you develop trust and build your relationship with your teen.

At the end of this book, you'll find resources to help you and your teen connect with the greater trans community and find the help you need to move forward. Most families don't go it alone. There's a world of support for you and your family, and by picking up this book, you've taken the first step toward that world.

CHAPTER 1

In the Beginning . . . There Were Also Trans People

Trans people have been in the media so much lately that it's easy to forget gender variance has existed for millennia. Remember the day your kid discovered Metallica and Prince? This is often how trans people your age feel when they hear trans identities described as a "trend" or "hot topic" in the news, or when the press focuses on recently out celebrities like Elliot Page or Tommy Dorfman even while less-famous trans activists have been doing world-changing work for decades under the mass media's radar.

In this chapter, we're going to talk about ways in which gender variance has appeared throughout history. We'll also talk about trans identities today and the progress the trans community has made in increasing trans visibility, gaining legal recognition, and making strides in trans health care. Finally, we'll talk about how various scientific disciplines have tried to study transgender identities (and some of the problems with this research).

Before we begin, I'd like to say a brief word about sources of information about gender identity. When teens come out as trans, everyone has their own way of finding information about what to do next: "Google it." "Ask my kid's pediatrician." "Find a group for trans parents." "Read a book." These can all be good solutions, but they're also easy ways to get misinformation. The first Google result isn't always an accurate one. Misleading material from anti-trans groups makes its way into places you might not expect. Books become outdated. When you're reading up on gender identity, always look at where your reading material comes from. If an article cites research, you may want to take a look at the research on your own. Information that comes from respected health-care organizations like the American Academy of Pediatrics and the World Professional Association for Transgender Health (WPATH) is more likely to be accurate than news articles or blogs. When in doubt, seek the viewpoints of trans people and read about their experiences.

A Brief History of Trans Identities

Most civilizations have some record of people who didn't conform to the male and female roles that have become standard
in the Western world today. Traditional Navajo culture has the
dilbaa', a person who might take on the role, clothing, and status
of a man, or mix traditional male attributes with female ones.
In ancient Rome, the emperor Elegabalus wore women's clothing, referred to herself as a "lady," removed her body hair, and
requested from surgeons what would be called gender-affirming
surgery today. In India, *hijra*—people assigned male at birth who
take on female social identities and sometimes modify their
bodies physically—have existed for centuries.

Although modern English words like *transgender* or *nonbinary* don't adequately describe these identities and cultural
roles, it's clear that examples of people who have gone beyond
male and female abound in many places and times. It's also true
that the way we tend to talk about gender today—as fixed categories assigned at birth, based solely on physical characteristics,
and occupying separate roles in society—isn't the way people
have always thought about gender everywhere in the world.

In the late 1800s, people who crossed gender lines started
to come to the attention of medical authorities and the emerging profession of psychiatry. In *Psychopathia Sexualis*, Richard
von Krafft-Ebing wrote about a patient who, despite seeming
outwardly male, felt the "constant feeling of being a woman from
top to toe" from a young age, and described feelings about her
physical appearance and social identity that we would likely call
gender dysphoria today. At the time, transgender identity was
seen as a medical or psychiatric disorder, and one that could
possibly be corrected—a practice that is still attempted in many
places today.

In 1923, Dr. Magnus Hirschfeld coined the German word
transsexualismus, which later became the English word *transsexual*. The term became widely used to describe people who

did not identify with their assigned gender at birth. Dr. Hirschfeld knew the common medical practice of trying to stop trans people from being trans was both inhumane and ineffective, and he formed the Institute for Sex Research, an organization that advocated for gender and sexual minorities in Berlin, Germany. The Institute conducted research that is still used today and developed some of the first gender-affirming medical procedures, while challenging the persecution transgender Germans faced and eventually, for a brief period, helping trans people win legal status in Germany.

Tragically, Dr. Hirschfeld was barred reentry to the country in 1932, and many of the staff and clients of the Institute were persecuted or killed by Nazis—who also literally burned much of the Institute's library and research on May 10, 1933. But they couldn't erase trans people. Some of the Institute's documents did survive, and they are some of the earliest records of trans people organizing, creating language to describe their experiences, and supporting one another. Although the trans community has made significant changes in how we talk and think about gender since that time, the Institute was one of the first places where gender-related health care was studied in an organized way.

Throughout the 20th century, trans people gained more legal protections and public recognition thanks to the sacrifices of trans activists who put their physical safety in danger to protest and riot against laws, police practices, and political oppression that limited their ability to live and work. At the same time, trans people increasingly began to connect to one another using newsletters and by gathering at community centers and conferences. Beginning in the 1950s, gender-affirming medical care became safer and easier to access as trans people and allies established programs at hospitals and clinics. In the 1990s and early 2000s, the internet made it easier for trans people to connect and share information, and the broader term *transgender* gradually began to replace *transsexual*.

Gender at Present

Over the past decade in the United States, accessing resources and support has become significantly easier for many trans people. With increased public visibility and greater legal protection, more people can live publicly as the gender with which they identify. A 2016 analysis of 32 studies from several countries estimated the number of people who identify as transgender at 355 out of every 100,000 people (or 0.355 percent).

Increased visibility in recent years has also resulted in political backlash. In the mid-2010s, several states enacted laws that attempted to restrict trans rights, from the use of public bathrooms to health care access. Conservative political groups have rallied around anti-trans laws, and many right-wing organizations began to promote the idea that trans people were dangerous or sick.

In June 2020, the United States Supreme Court issued a 6–3 decision in *Bostock v. Clayton County*, a case brought on behalf of three people—two gay, one transgender—who had been fired from their jobs when their employers learned of their identities. The court ruled that the 1964 Civil Rights Act protected both gay and transgender employees because of its prohibitions against sex discrimination. Legal scholars predict this ruling may have applications beyond employment because of other federal statutes that prohibit sex discrimination in housing, education, and health care.

Today, trans people are organizing widely to create change and provide community resources. Organizations like the National Center for Transgender Equality (NCTE) advocate policy change around issues important to trans people. The WPATH promotes quality trans health care globally. Black and Pink is a prison abolitionist organization that fights to improve conditions for trans and queer incarcerated people across the United States. Many smaller organizations have led the way in driving policy changes and providing direct aid, such as New York's Audre Lorde Project and TransLatina Coalition in Los Angeles.

You might wonder what any of this means for your family. It means that you and your teen have the opportunity not only to benefit from the actions of people who have fought for trans recognition, but also to continue the fight. Any contribution you make—on a small level, like advocating for safer bathrooms at your teen's summer camp, or on a larger level, like policy advocacy in your city—has the potential to make life easier for trans teens today and for the generations that come after them.

Questions You Might Be Afraid to Ask: Why Does It Seem Like So Many People Are Coming Out as Transgender?

Seeing more and more people publicly coming out as trans might make you wonder why it's so common now. You probably don't remember going to school with any out trans kids, and although you might remember Elton John or Ellen DeGeneres coming out as gay, you certainly don't remember many (or any) openly trans celebrities when you were growing up. You might even have questions like, "Is this just a fad? Are all these people really trans, or are they just jumping on the bandwagon?"

It's important to remember that the increased acceptance and awareness of trans identities that the world has experienced in recent years has had a dramatic effect on the ability of trans people to discover their identities and come out publicly. If you were a trans teen in the 1990s, 1970s, or 1950s, how would you have known you were trans, or that your feelings were shared by other people? With almost no media about trans people available to the average person, where would you have found that information?

Suppose you did happen upon a mimeographed trans news-letter, or found out about a clinic in your city for trans people. And suppose you did use those resources to figure out your identity. Would you have been brave enough to live openly as your identified gender? And if you were, would you let your friends and neighbors know you were trans? What about your boss?

Consider that innovative French surgeon Georges Burou reported performing 3,000 gender-affirming surgeries on trans women between 1956 and 1973. How many of these women could safely announce their identities in public at that time without fear of violence or discrimination? The magazine *Transgender Tapestry* had thousands of paid subscribers between 1979 and 2006. Have you ever seen an issue?

In fact, you've likely met trans people who simply weren't open about it, or who weren't able to express their gender identities out of fear. The older member of your church who just came out as a trans woman may have spent decades hiding who she was. You might have had nonbinary neighbors you didn't notice. On any morning, you might have sat next to me on the subway and had no idea you were shoulder to shoulder with a trans person, foggy with sleep and sipping a to-go coffee just like you.

It's also much more acceptable to portray trans lives in the media than it used to be. Think back to Ellen DeGeneres in the 1990s: Advertisers pulled their ads from her show and the network started running a viewer discretion warning after her character came out as gay. With that in mind, how much harder do you think it would have been to create a show with a trans main character at that time? Trans stigma also meant that trans actors, writers, and directors didn't have many career opportunities. In other words, the lack of trans visibility doesn't mean trans people didn't exist; it means you weren't seeing them because media companies didn't want to take on the risk.

Parenting Tips and Conversation Starters: Global Strategies for Approaching Gender with Your Teen

Starting a conversation with your teen about gender identity might seem daunting. You might have so many questions that you're not sure where to start. Or you might not even be sure what your questions are. These tips can help you have a more productive, enlightening conversation:

- **Use the Ring Theory.** Susan Silk and Barry Goldman came up with what they call the "Ring Theory," which is a strategy to prioritize someone who is experiencing an intense emotional event while still honoring your own feelings. Here's how it works:

  First, make a dot in the center of a piece of paper. That's your teen. Draw a circle around it. In that circle are the people closest to your teen: you and your teen's other caregivers, siblings, close family members, and closest friends. Draw another circle. In that circle are the people more peripheral to your teen's life: teachers, neighbors, acquaintances, and relatives who aren't as close. Draw a third circle. In that circle are the people who are strangers to your teen: the people in your triathlon club, your own therapist, and other parents you might meet online. Your diagram can have as many rings as you like and prioritize relationships according to your teen's circumstances; the important thing is that they're ordered by importance of their relationship to your teen.

  The person in the center is the one most in need of comfort, safety, and allyship from the people in the first ring, then the second ring, and so on. The rule here is "comfort *in*, dump *out*." If you're feeling difficult or painful emotions about your teen's gender identity, that's okay—just take those troubles to someone in your ring or the rings outside it, not to your teen at the center. This practice also gives you permission to set boundaries with the people in the outer rings: "Sorry, neighbor-I-barely-see, but your 'concern' about my kid wearing a dress is way out of line."

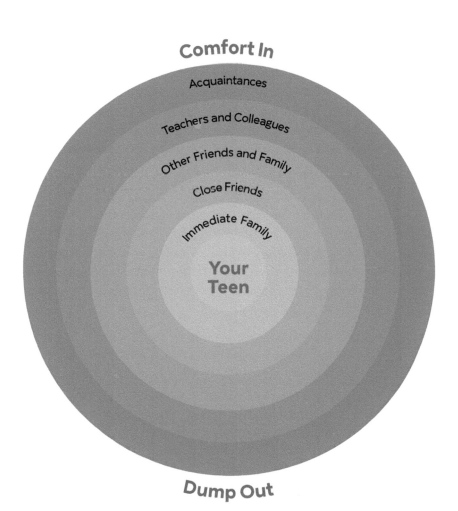

- **Emphasize the Positive.** In the *New York Times,* Dr. Paria Hassouri, a pediatrician and the mother of a trans teen, wrote about the atmosphere of anxiety that can sometimes develop in a family of a teen who comes out as transgender. You might worry about future bullying or job discrimination as a form of support—*shouldn't* you be looking out for your kids?—but by doing so, you might be making your teen's environment more negative than it needs to be. Hassouri notes:

  Your child is dealing with enough negativity from the media and outside world. Make your home a safe space. Don't be a pessimist. Instead of telling your child they have a long and limited road ahead, tell them their future is bright with no limits on what they can accomplish or who they can be.

  When you're thinking about voicing a worry you have about your teen's future, think about why you're saying what you're about to say. Is it helpful to your teen? Or do you just feel like you need to get it out? Consider talking to a friend instead. Talk about your teen's future in positive terms, focusing on their strengths and ambitions rather than on your own fears.

- **Find Positive Stories.** What kinds of stories about trans people do you have in your head? If you don't know a lot of trans people, your picture of what a trans person's life looks like might come from TV or movies. Unfortunately, a lot of people who tell stories about trans people are only interested in the negative parts—death, discrimination, and family rejection—or only focus on transition instead of representing trans people as whole individuals with interesting lives.

Fortunately, there are plenty of trans creators telling stories of their own. Read a book or watch a film or TV show about trans people created *by* trans people, either by yourself or with your teen. (There are quite a few listed in the Resources section, page 126.)

The Science Behind Gender

You might have heard people say that sex and gender are different things. Although an analysis of the meanings of *sex* and *gender* throughout history is probably more than you signed up for when you bought this book, people usually use *sex* to refer to people's physical bodies—the chromosomes, genitals, and other features that make the doctor write "M" or "F" on your birth certificate. And we usually use *gender* to mean someone's inner sense of identity: the way you know what gender you are in your head no matter what the rest of your body looks like. (We'll get to other terms like *gender role* and *gender expression* in the next chapter.)

But it's a little more complicated than brain versus body. After all, the brain *is* part of the body, and the same factors that affect the development of the rest of the body can affect the brain. As biology researcher Milton Diamond notes, the brain and other parts of the body develop at separate times, leaving open the possibility that the brain may be changed by hormones during fetal development but the rest of the body may not visibly be affected (as it is with intersex conditions, where anatomy at birth is not easily categorized into binary sex). Some research suggests that genetics may also have some effect. Studies on the brains of trans people of various ages, both with and without gender-affirming hormone therapy, have shown these brains to have similarities, on average, to those of their identified gender.

However, it's still impossible to know if someone is trans by looking at their brain. And we already have a perfectly good (and empirically validated) way of figuring out whether someone is trans: asking them about their experiences of their identity and body. Science philosopher Anna K. Swartz points out that this research on brain gender may end up marginalizing trans youth further, forcing trans patients to submit to invasive medical testing in order to access treatment, or to conversion therapy to attempt to change their brains.

We don't know exactly why gender variance exists. It's likely to be more complicated than a single gene or a tiny amount of cortical thickness. The interplay between biology and environment can be staggeringly complex. Reducing trans identity to what we can detect in the brain with the technology we have right now would be a mistake. The question we should be asking is not *What physical differences can we find in trans people's brains?* but *What does research tell us about what we should do after a teenager tells us they're transgender—regardless of where that identity comes from?*

It is a crucial distinction. We aren't 100 percent sure what causes dyslexia either, but that doesn't stop us from developing educational support to help dyslexic kids thrive in school. Similarly, we can't pinpoint exactly why some people identify as trans or predict someone's gender identity from an MRI, but we do know from the research we have that affirming trans teens leads to better outcomes than denying them the ability to express their gender.

Just as important, we also know that trans people who can access gender-affirming medical treatment lead far happier lives than those who cannot. In the next section, we'll talk about some of this research.

Recent Discoveries of Note

When trans identities first came to the attention of health and mental health professionals and researchers more than a century ago, no one knew exactly how to respond. Clinicians treating trans people had to weigh the risks and benefits of gender-affirming treatment without knowing exactly what the long-term effects might be. So did the trans people being treated. Philosophical questions came up: *Who gets to decide what medical procedures trans people undergo? How much risk is too much risk? What do we do when we can't predict exactly what will happen?* Understandably, many trans people became frustrated that there were so many barriers to getting gender-affirming care, and that health-care professionals often didn't believe that trans people should be in charge of their own bodies.

Fortunately, since then, we've accumulated a great deal of research that indicates that listening to trans people about their own lives and bodies creates better outcomes. In 2018, researchers at the What We Know Project at Cornell University conducted a review of the past 25 years of research on gender affirmation in trans people and concluded that "gender transition, including medical treatments such as hormone therapy and surgeries, improves the overall well-being of transgender individuals."

Everything we've figured out so far about trans health and mental health points to the idea that affirming your teen's gender is likely to have a positive effect, with few apparent risks. Turn to the tips on page 15 ("Understanding Your Teen's Unique Experiences with Gender Identity") to find out more about how to understand and affirm your teen.

Questions You Might Be Afraid to Ask: If Gender Is a Construct, Why Do People Transition?

It's true that many aspects of what we call *gender* are socially constructed and not innate, fixed qualities that men and women have. Ideas like "men like to repair stuff" and "women enjoy caring for kids" aren't based on anything we know about the human brain but rather on tradition and socialization. And our traditions about what people should wear, think, eat, and do based on their gender have varied greatly throughout history. We call these ideas *gender roles* or *gender norms*.

But that doesn't mean gender roles are exactly the same thing as gender identity. It's hard to define exactly what constitutes *identity*—this isn't a philosophy or psychology textbook!—but it appears to go much deeper than whether you like earrings or watch sports. Most trans people report a strong sense of internal difference from others—often from an early age—that goes beyond stuff like clothes and hobbies. For some, this experience includes strong feelings about changing their physical bodies, not just their social role or pronouns. Research on trans brains and brain gender is in its infancy, but it's possible that biology plays a strong role.

You might ask: *If gender identity isn't the same as gender role, why do trans people socially transition? Why start wearing different clothes or styling your hair differently if you don't need those things to be your identified gender?* Think about these questions for a moment, then answer this: Why do *you* wear the clothes you wear?

One of the realities of life is that virtually everywhere in the world, people expect you to look a certain way based on your gender. If you don't, you might get mistaken for the wrong gender. Or people might make fun of you. For many trans (and cis) people, being seen as their identified gender is important. Many trans teens find it hard to get others to accept their gender, and clothes and hair can provide visual cues. And for some teens, coming out as trans provides an opportunity to wear clothes, makeup, and hairstyles that they might have wanted to wear before, but weren't "allowed" to.

But not all trans people dress or act in a gender-stereotypical way. Some trans people embrace the idea that your inner identity, not your clothes or social role, is what defines your gender. There are plenty of transfeminine people who don't dress in an overtly "femme" way and many transmasculine people who wear makeup—just like the many cis people who bend the "rules" of gender.

For some trans teens, clothing can present a double bind: "If I look too feminine, people say I'm trying too hard. If I don't, people say I'm not trying hard enough, or that I'm not 'really' a girl!" Avoid putting pressure on your teen to look a certain way. They're getting enough pressure from the rest of the world!

Parenting Tips and Conversation Starters: Understanding Your Teen's Unique Experiences with Gender Identity

As you've probably figured out, trans people's experiences with gender differ greatly from person to person. Just as your experiences in your own gender—including your relationship with your body, clothes, and social role—are unique, your teen has a relationship with their gender that is all their own. Here are some ways to start a conversation about your teen's gender experiences:

- **Ask the Right Questions.** Forget not knowing what to say—you might not even know what questions to ask! Here are some questions to get you started on understanding more about what your teen is experiencing:

  → "Can you tell me a little more about what that means to you?"

  → "Is there anything you'd recommend I read or watch that might help me understand what you're going through?"

  → "I don't think I fully understand that word. Can you tell me more about it, or point me to some information?"

  → "What kind of language do you need me to use?"

  → "Do you want me to tell anyone right now?"

  → "What do you feel like you need to change to express your gender?"

  → "What should I call you?"

  → "What can I do to help?"

  → "Is there anything I've been doing that you wish I'd stop doing?"

- **Question or Statement? Know the Difference.** Sometimes parental concern can come across as invalidation. Your concerns might be perfectly understandable—*What's your future going to look like? Aren't you afraid of getting bullied? What are the risks of medical intervention?*—but the way you express them might be heard as discouraging or dismissive.

Before you ask a question, think about why you're asking it. What information do you need to support your teen? Are you asking this question to deepen your understanding, or are you trying to dispel your own anxieties? Is the question really a statement about what you think your teen should do?

In resolving family conflict, therapists Drs. John and Julie Gottman recommend asking open-ended questions and postponing talking about your own wishes and feelings until you fully understand the other person's feelings. Here are some suggestions for questions to ask:

Question: Aren't there a lot of risks to hormone therapy?

Try Instead: Do you have any information I can read about hormone therapy?

Question: You never showed any signs of being trans—why now?

Try Instead: Tell me about how you figured this out about yourself.

Question: Don't you want to wait until you're older?

Try Instead: Tell me more about why this is so important to you right now.

- **Get Halfway There.** A recent study showed that trans teenagers rated their parents as more supportive than the parents rated themselves. And when asked about what aspects of family support mattered the most, teenagers said that just acknowledging their identity by using the right name and pronouns was the most important thing their parents did. Ironically, though, the parents in the study reported that names and pronouns were what caused them the most trouble!

This is great news for family members who want to be supportive but don't fully understand trans identities or feel 100 percent certain about how to move forward. I often tell parents that using their teen's name and pronouns is the "free space" of parenting. It costs nothing and involves no permanent changes, but it tells your teen you're willing to listen and support them. Chapter 2 (page 27) provides more information about trans-affirming language.

Fluid? A Spectrum? Why Gender Is Complicated

If you've ever heard your teen say "gender is a spectrum," you may have wondered exactly what they meant. Although the ways people experience gender can be complex and nuanced, it boils down to something pretty simple: gender identity isn't just "male" or "female."

Many people's gender identities fall between those two binary categories. Although not every trans person identifies somewhere between male and female—in fact, plenty of trans people's identities are on the extreme ends of the male-female spectrum—people who identify this way often describe themselves as *nonbinary, genderqueer,* or some other label that isn't wholly male or female. And many other trans people feel that their identities exist somewhere outside of male and female categories altogether, or don't feel a particularly strong sense of gender identity at all. These people also may identify with nonbinary labels, and sometimes call themselves *genderless or agender.* We'll talk a little bit more about these labels in chapter 2 (page 27).

Some people describe their gender identity as *fluid.* This means their gender identity shifts or changes over time. They may feel more male or more female on one day, or experience a mix of masculine and feminine identities on another. They may use different pronouns on different days. Or their gender identity might evolve over months or years.

Gender identity isn't the only aspect of gender that can be fluid or exist on a spectrum. The same is true of gender *expression*. Many people's gender expression exists between the extremes of the gender spectrum, or changes from day to day, often for different reasons. Some people feel more masculine or feminine from day to day. Some dress differently depending on who they're going to see later (especially if they're worried about their safety). Others dress in a mix of masculine and feminine clothes—or just go with whatever's clean. This is true of both cis and trans people.

What Does Gender Expression Mean for Your Teen?

You may have noticed that your teen's gender expression changes from day to day or doesn't line up with what you'd expect from their identified gender. Questions may have popped into your mind: *Does his skirt mean that he doesn't identify as male anymore? Does her buzz cut mean I should stop using she/her pronouns? What, exactly, does a choker mean?*

Trans teens are no different from cis teens in that they need space to experiment with different looks and wear what makes them most comfortable, even if it isn't exactly what you'd expect from their identified or assigned gender. They might also try out different labels or pronouns to see what fits best. In your role as a parent, you can help your teen by reserving judgment and refraining from making assumptions. Keep using the name, gender labels, and pronouns they've asked you to use, and know that these identifiers might change as they grow more comfortable with their identity.

Questions You Might Be Afraid to Ask: What if This Is Just a Phase?

This is a question I get from a lot of parents. Many are afraid that their teen will someday realize they don't identify as trans anymore, or that their teen may regret socially transitioning or receiving gender-affirming medical care.

Luckily, there's been plenty of research on this subject that shows trans youth who socially transition or receive gender-affirming medical care demonstrate improved mental health and quality of life. By some measures, socially or medically affirmed youth demonstrate no greater distress than cisgender youth. This reduction in mental health symptoms and gender dysphoria also appears to hold true for adults who receive gender-affirming care.

Some parents worry that identifying as trans may be a "trend" of recent years, or that their teens might do so to fit in with friends. The available research suggests otherwise. A study at a major gender clinic showed that, although the number of trans teens presenting to the clinic increased between 2000 and 2016, teens referred to the clinic in recent years did not seem to present differently from those arriving at the clinic in earlier years in terms of gender dysphoria intensity or psychological characteristics, and they were no more likely to stop treatment. The most likely explanation for the increase in gender clinic referrals is that adolescents are more likely to recognize that they are transgender, not that being trans is trendy. (Indeed, ask any trans youth and they'll tell you that being trans in high school is far from easy.) Turn to page 6 ("Why Does it Seem Like So Many People Are Coming Out as Transgender?") for more information on why you might feel like you're seeing more trans people these days.

Other parents worry that their teens will eventually *detransition*, or return to living as their assigned gender again.

However, detransition is actually very rare, both in adolescents and adults.

In a study of thousands of youth referred to a gender clinic in the Netherlands between 2000 and 2016, only 1.9 percent of those who began puberty blockers stopped this treatment (although it's impossible to say whether they stopped treatment because they detransitioned or for other reasons). In a large-scale survey of transgender adults, 8 percent of all respondents reported detransitioning at any point, and only 0.4 percent of the overall sample reported detransitioning because they'd realized transition wasn't right for them. The rest said they'd detransitioned because of pressure from parents or other family members, harassment, job discrimination, or other reasons. The majority of those who stated they'd detransitioned (62 percent) had already retransitioned at the time of the survey.

This information may help you understand why the consensus among medical and mental health professionals is to provide adolescents with gender-affirming care and allow them to socially transition. The American Medical Association, the American Academy of Pediatrics, the American Psychological Association, the American Psychiatric Association, the American Academy of Child and Adolescent Psychiatry, and dozens of other major professional organizations have endorsed gender-affirming care for transgender youth.

It's also important to remember the risks of *not* intervening. This is where cognitive biases come into play. People considering medical interventions often assign more weight to the risks of the intervention than to the risks of non-intervention. This means that you might be more afraid of the relatively small risk of seeking gender-affirming care for your child than the relatively large risk of not doing so, even if your child is in serious distress or experiencing irreversible body changes that medical intervention such as puberty blockers could halt or delay.

$\longrightarrow$

Remember that your teen will not get surgery or hormones overnight. For teens, these changes invariably involve seeing a mental health professional trained in the assessment of trans adolescents. For most teens, social transition is the first step. Fortunately, there are no known side effects of gender exploration or social transition, and many psychological benefits.

Parenting Tips and Conversation Starters: Creating an Open Dialogue with Your Teen

You might find that your teen is reluctant to talk to you about their experiences of being transgender. It may not have anything to do with your parenting or the way you've handled finding out about their gender identity. Your teen might be experiencing any number of feelings about having come out to you: embarrassment, fear, anxiety, or just plain old awkwardness. Here are some tips for helping your teen feel more comfortable talking about their gender:

- **Give Them Space *Not* to Talk.** It might seem counter-intuitive, but by respecting their wishes—even if those wishes seem to involve retreating under a pile of blankets when you bring up gender—you will create more trust and lessen their anxiety.

- **Check Back In without Pushing Too Hard.** Just because they don't want to talk now doesn't mean they'll never want to talk. Have patience and find a quiet, private time to have the conversation when you're both feeling less anxiety.

- **Think about Reasons They Might Not Be Opening Up.** Maybe you haven't always talked about trans people in an affirming way, or maybe gender and sexuality have always been fraught subjects in your house. It's not too late to correct the perceptions your teen might have of your willingness to listen and affirm them. Saying something like "I realize I might have gotten some things wrong" won't cause your teen to think any less of you. Showing the ability to admit your mistakes will help your teen see you as a real, vulnerable human being.

- **Start Using the Language Your Teen Is Using to Describe Their Gender.** Doing so may lessen any fear that you won't understand what they're talking about, or that you'll invalidate their experiences. The next chapter covers trans-affirming language.

Key Takeaways

In this chapter, we talked about the basics of gender: what it is, where it comes from, and what it might mean to your teen. As you engage with your teen, keep the following in mind:

- Throughout history and across civilizations, many people haven't conformed to the male and female roles that have become standard in the Western world today.

- In recent years, trans people have been increasingly able to live publicly as their identified gender because of increased resources, support, and legal protections as well as safer and more accessible medical care.

- You can help create a positive environment for your teen by using the ring theory, emphasizing the positive, and focusing on media about trans people that is created by trans people.

- Research shows that affirming trans teens leads to better outcomes than denying them the ability to express their gender.

- Gender isn't binary! It exists along (and outside of!) a spectrum, and your teen's understanding of their gender may change over time.

- Some important ways to show support for your teen include asking the right questions, acknowledging their identity by using their identified name and pronouns, and creating an open dialogue.

In the next chapter, we'll get into more of the practical details of what to do when your teen comes out to you as trans. We'll go over key terminology, discuss the different aspects of gender identity, talk about pronouns and how to use them, and explore how to affirm your teen's choice of name socially and legally.

Although you've only finished the first chapter, you might feel overwhelmed with information right now. That's totally normal. Just like other aspects of parenting—like the terrible twos, or figuring out what to do when your kid calls you a butthole—none of this stuff comes naturally to most people. It's going to involve some tough decisions and a big learning curve. But don't worry! I'll be with you every step of the way.

CHAPTER 2

When *They* Means One: A Primer on Inclusive Language

You probably picked up this book because you're looking to build your ability to support your teen in the way they need to be supported. Using the language your teen asks you to use and learning about the ways people describe and experience gender identity are two of the strongest, most lasting ways of communicating to your teen that you support and affirm them.

In this chapter, we'll talk about the most common words your teen might use to describe basic gender concepts, identity labels, feelings they have about gender, and the way they express their gender. I'll answer common questions about language, like how to use gender-neutral pronouns and what makes gender identity different from sexual orientation. We'll also talk about how to use validating language to have the kinds of conversations that strengthen the bond between you and your teen.

I often hear parents say things like "I'm never going to get it right." I don't believe that! Plenty of people use the right names and pronouns for one another with no apparent trouble. Those people don't have telepathy or extra-special language-learning powers. We struggle with new words and concepts just like everyone else. But we put in the work of learning (and practicing!) the right language for one another because we know it's important to the people we care about. This chapter will give you some ideas about how you can do that, too.

Transgender? Genderfluid? Nonbinary? Understanding Different Labels

If you've ever googled the word *transgender,* you've probably unearthed tens or hundreds of words used to describe gender. There are words for broad concepts, like *gender identity.* There are words for identities, like *transfeminine* or *agender,* and words for activities or experiences, like *drag* or *dysphoria.* The deluge of words might be intimidating. You might wonder why you need to understand so many words to understand your teen when gender used to seem simple to you.

For many reasons, the English language has more words about gender than it used to have. People in different places, times, and cultures have come up with various, often overlapping words to describe similar things. Terminology becomes outdated, and newer, more precise words replace older, less accurate ones. And people come up with smaller, more fine-tuned labels to describe experiences we used to describe using broader terms.

It doesn't mean you have to go on the internet and memorize every gender-related word you can find. Although it's helpful to learn basic terms, knowing every bit of trans terminology your teen knows is not necessary. The most important thing you can do is be curious about your teen's personal experiences.

Dictionary definitions can only tell you what the larger trans community means when they use a particular word or phrase. But a dictionary can't tell you what that word means to your teen. For that reason, it's important to use the terms your teen uses to describe their own experiences, even if you know of other words for those experiences.

Here are some basic terms you can use to talk about gender with your teen:

Gender identity or *identified gender* is your inner sense of what your gender is—male, female, something else, or nothing at all. Everyone has one, including you.

Your *gender expression* is the outward stuff, like clothes, hair, and pronouns. It's not the same thing as gender identity. Your gender expression doesn't have to match the stereotypes of your identified gender. For example, many women—trans and cis—have short hair and shop in the men's section, but that doesn't make them men.

Labels like *transgender* and *cisgender* (often shortened to *trans* and *cis*) describe whether your gender assigned at birth—that is, the "M" or "F" on your birth certificate—matches the way you identify yourself now. A transgender person's gender is different from the one assigned to them at birth, while a cisgender person's is the same. Some anti-trans activists have tried to advance the idea that *cis* is a negative word or a slur. However, most people consider *cis* and *cisgender* to be neutral descriptors of someone's gender history just like *trans* or *transgender*, with no negative connotations about the value of either cis or trans people.

Gender dysphoria describes a sense of discomfort with one's body, appearance, or social identity. Not all trans people feel that this term describes their experiences with their gender characteristics. A related term is *gender euphoria*, the feeling of being comfortable in one's body or social identity. Many trans teens experience gender euphoria when they're able to affirm their gender with social or physical changes, or when others recognize them as their identified gender.

Transmasculine is an umbrella term that describes someone who was assigned female at birth and identifies as male, masculine, or something else. *Transfeminine* describes someone who was assigned male at birth and identifies as female, feminine, or something else. Some people use terms like *female-to-male* (*FTM*) or *male-to-female* (*MTF*), and others consider those terms outdated and inaccurate, especially if they feel that they have always been their identified gender.

Some identities fall outside the gender binary, while others exist within it. Someone whose gender is labeled as *binary* identifies as fully male or female. A *nonbinary* person identifies somewhere in between—or entirely outside of—male and female identities. Identity labels often overlap with other labels. For example, many trans people also identify as nonbinary.

Terms like *agender* or *genderless* describe someone who has no sense of gender, does not identify strongly as any gender, or thinks of gender as unimportant. A *genderfluid* person's gender identity or expression may shift and change at different times.

Terms like *gender variant, gender diverse,* and *gender atypical* describe people whose gender identity or expression is outside the norm. Most people don't use these terms as identity labels. Instead, they're broad terms that capture the experiences of many people with many different identities. Some people use the term *genderqueer* as an identity label, which is a broad term that means different things to different people, but usually means something like "having a gender identity or expression that is not typical."

You've probably also heard of *drag queens/kings, crossdressers,* and other people who aren't necessarily transgender but whose communities and identities often overlap. A *drag queen* or *drag king* is an entertainer who performs as a woman or man in a bar, stage show, or pageant, usually with over-the-top, exaggerated costumes and makeup. *Don't use these terms as synonyms for* transgender. Being a drag queen/king doesn't necessarily mean you're trans or that you identify with the gender of your drag persona, and cis or trans people of any gender can do drag.

A *cross-dresser* is someone (most often a cisgender man) who dresses like the opposite gender for fun, comfort, or sexual reasons. Trans people who wear clothes typical of their identified gender aren't cross-dressing—they're just dressing. Never use this term to refer to someone who doesn't use it themself.

So Your Teen Is Transgender

What does it mean to be transgender—other than identifying as something different from what's on your birth certificate? In other words, what is your teen *actually* saying about themself when they say, "I'm transgender"?

In the broadest terms, transgender people feel as though their assigned gender does not capture who they are. But every trans person experiences these feelings differently. You may have heard some trans people describe feeling as though they were "born in the wrong body." This is true for some trans people, but not all. Others don't feel alienated from their bodies but feel a strong pull toward a different body type, set of characteristics, or social identity. Some people feel disconnected from certain parts of their physical bodies, but not others. And many feel as though they don't need to change their bodies but rather their outward gender expression or social identity.

Sound vague? That's because trans experiences are vast and diverse, and there are as many ways of describing the trans experience as there are trans people. It's probably not going to be helpful for you to know exactly what every trans person might mean when they say "I'm trans." And—luckily—you don't have to. Although it's helpful to read about trans experiences and listen to trans voices, your number-one job is to listen to what your teen is saying when they describe how they feel about their own gender.

For many teens, being transgender might mean *doing* something: changing the way they look or present themselves. Some people use the word *transition* to refer to this experience, while others use the term *gender affirmation*. Your teen might need *social gender transition/affirmation* (changes in one's name, pronouns, hair, clothes, or other outward indicators of gender) or *medical gender transition/affirmation* (body changes like hormone therapy or surgery made with the help of a health-care professional).

But being trans might not mean any of those things for your teen right now, or only some of those things. Not every trans person makes or wants to make physical changes to their body. Not every trans person is ready to come out to everyone right away. Every trans person has gender affirmation needs that are different from what another trans person might need. These needs may change over time as your teen explores what being trans means to them.

So Your Teen Identifies as Something You Don't Understand

What if your teen comes to you with a term or label that isn't anywhere in this book? Maybe you're frantically flipping through the index or googling what your teen just told you. Or maybe what they mean by *nonbinary* or *genderfluid* is different to them than what you assumed it meant.

That's fine. You don't get it. They probably didn't expect you to get it. So own up to the fact that you don't get it. Know that your teen told you about their identity for a good reason: because they trust you and feel like this information is as important to you as it is to them.

You might be afraid to ask questions that might make you sound ignorant or out-of-touch, especially after that time your teen made fun of you for calling their PlayStation "the Nintendo." Or maybe you're worried about respecting your teen's privacy now that they're older. However, given the fact that they told you in the first place, they likely want you to be interested in their experiences. In fact, I've heard more complaints from young clients about their parents *not* being curious about what they're going through.

Turn to page 16 ("Ask the Right Questions") to learn about open-ended questions you can ask your teen to find out more about their identity and how to support them, or to page 36 ("How to Use Validating Language to Talk to Your Teen about Gender Identity") to learn about how you can validate your child's experiences.

Questions You Might Be Afraid to Ask: If My Teen Is Transgender, Does That Also Mean They're Gay?

Not necessarily! Labels like *gay* and *straight* describe sexual orientation; that is, the gender or genders you're attracted to. Labels like *transgender* and *nonbinary* describe gender identity: the gender you are, regardless of who you'd like to date. Although some labels encompass both gender identity and sexuality—like *queer*, which means "having a gender identity *and/or* sexuality that's different from the norm"—most identity labels refer to one or the other.

Trans people can have any sexual orientation that cis people can have: gay, straight, bisexual, pansexual, asexual, or anything else. Having a particular sexual orientation doesn't have anything to do with the validity of your gender. For example, being attracted to women doesn't make a woman (trans or cis) any less of a woman.

One reason parents often get confused about the difference between gender identity and sexual orientation is stereotypes about people who aren't straight. Often, gay men and lesbians are stereotyped as having feminine or masculine gender expressions—which is certainly true of some, but not all. As we discussed earlier, gender *expression* isn't the same as gender *identity*, which means that feminine mannerisms in a man don't mean that he wants people to see him as a woman, for example.

Another reason parents get confused is that the larger queer community includes people who use many different labels, some of which are related to sexual orientation and some of which are related to gender identity or expression. Trans and cis people in the queer community might share common spaces and activities, like support groups or Pride events. This might seem confusing to an outsider—*Why stick together when you're all so different?*—but it's less about being exactly the same and more about having shared experiences, goals, and history.

Some teens come to a different understanding of their sexual orientation as they begin to understand their gender. Many trans people don't figure out their attractions until they're comfortable with their bodies, secure in their identities, or out to the world. As with any other teen, a trans teen might adopt different labels to see what fits. Or they might not use any labels at all.

It's important to use the labels your teen uses for their own gender identity and sexual orientation. Always ask rather than assume. And don't use language for sexual orientation that invalidates your teen's gender—for example, a trans teen boy who dates boys would probably not identify himself as straight, and labeling him that way might make him feel like you see him as a girl.

Parenting Tips and Conversation Starters: How to Use Validating Language to Talk to Your Teen about Gender Identity

When you found out your teen was questioning their gender, it was likely the start of a series of conversations about what that meant. Maybe these were good conversations and both of you came away feeling understood. Or maybe your teen said something surprising to you, like, "You don't get it!" or "It's not easy to talk to you about these things."

Having *validating language* in your toolbox might make these conversations easier. Validating your teen doesn't mean you always agree with everything they're saying or never set boundaries. It means that you treat their concerns as understandable and important, even—especially—if you don't fully understand where they're coming from.

At its core, *validation* is just language that helps your teen understand that their needs are important to you and that you can understand how they feel:

- "I can see why you were upset!"

- "It makes sense that you'd feel that way."

Reflection means summarizing information your teen has told you without judging or criticizing:

- "So they told you they wouldn't call you 'Malcolm'?"

- "It sounds like you're having a lot of trouble making this decision."

Normalizing is telling your teen that they're not alone in what they're going through:

- "If my friend said that, I'd be mad, too."

- "That's not weird at all! A lot of people freeze up when someone asks them a sensitive question."

Support is anything you say to offer help or guidance:

- "What would you like me to do?"

- "Please come to me if you need to talk."

On the other hand, a lot of words that might come to your mind first can be seen as *invalidating*, even if you don't mean them that way. Here are some traps to avoid.

Minimizing means making your teen's concerns seem small or unimportant:

- "Are you sure you're not overreacting?"

- "I don't see why it's so important to you."

- "You need to get your priorities in order."

Siding with others can make it seem like everyone else's perspective is more important to you than your teen's:

- "I'm sure your coach just wants what's best for the team."

- "Mrs. Morgan has known you for so long as a boy. Just put yourself in her shoes."

Toxic positivity is when you imply that it's not okay to talk about negative emotions or accept the reality of bad situations:

- "You just need to have hope that things will get better at school."

- "Don't waste your energy being upset."

Negativity might come in the form of framing transgender lives as sad, negative, or worse than cisgender ones:

- "You're going down a really hard road."

- "What if no one wants to hire you?"

You'll also want to avoid *asking your child to support you*:

- "I find this whole thing so confusing. Can't you just be understanding?"

- "I need to talk to you about how hard your transition has been on me."

If you're in need of support, turn to the Resources section on page 126 to learn about places to find it.

What Are Pronouns and How Do I Use Them?

A *pronoun* is a part of speech used as a substitute for a noun. In the phrase "I lost my hat when the wind blew it off," I'm using *it* as a pronoun, substituting it for the word *hat*.

Personal pronouns refer to people: *his* bicycle, *their* house, *she* runs. In English, as in most languages, personal pronouns are gendered. In other words, unless you're using a gender-neutral pronoun like *they*, pronouns indicate the gender of the person you're talking about. Your teen might want you to start using new personal pronouns for them as they begin to explore their gender.

How do we decide what pronouns to use for someone? Your default is probably to go by their appearance. But pronouns are not always obvious. Someone who looks feminine isn't always going to go by *she*, and masculine people don't all go by *he*. And you don't need to look androgynous to go by a gender-neutral pronoun. If you're not sure what pronouns someone uses, it's a good idea to refrain from using pronouns at all until you can ask them.

In this section, we'll talk about the different types of pronouns (gendered and gender-neutral), other ways that language can be gendered or gender-neutral, and what to do if you mess up.

One final note: You may have heard the phrase *preferred pronouns*. Many trans people feel that this phrase shouldn't be used because the word *preferred* implies that trans people's pronouns are optional or less legitimate than cis people's pronouns. In other words, your pronouns aren't just preferred—they're your pronouns, period. In this book, I'll be using the word *pronouns* by itself.

Understanding Gender-Neutral Language

Some trans people use gender-neutral language to refer to themselves, including *gender-neutral pronouns*: pronouns that don't indicate the gender of the person being referred to. *They* is a common gender-neutral pronoun used by many people who don't use *he* or *she*. *They* is also commonly used to refer to people whose gender is unknown—for example, "When we hire a dog walker, they'll need to be available on Fridays." We'll talk about different gender-neutral pronouns a little bit more in the next section, but very briefly, some other pronouns you might hear include *xe/xyr* and *ze/zir* (both pronounced the same way) and *em/eir* (pronounced like *them/their*, but without the "th" sound).

However, gender-neutral language doesn't stop at pronouns. Many of the words we use for relationships, forms of address, or job titles are gendered—like *boyfriend* or *waitress*. If your teen or someone you know uses gender-neutral pronouns, here's a guide to some gender-neutral terms to go along with them.

GENDERED TERM	GENDER-NEUTRAL TERM
Boyfriend/girlfriend	Date, sweetheart, significant other, partner
Brother/sister	Sibling
Husband/wife	Spouse, partner, significant other
Mr./Ms.	Mx. (pronounced "mix")
Niece/nephew	Nibling
Son/daughter, grandson/ granddaughter	Child, kid, grandchild, grandkid
Waiter/waitress, actor/ actress, businessman/ businesswoman, etc.	Sometimes, traditionally male terms are also gender neutral (e.g., *actor*); other times, neutral terms (e.g., *mail carrier, firefighter, server*) are available

Remember that not all trans people use gender-neutral language for themselves. Many trans people use gendered language and pronouns, so make sure to ask first before assuming a trans person is "Mx. Smith" instead of "Mr." or "Ms. Smith," or "they" instead of "she" or "he." Some people don't use pronouns at all, preferring that people just use their names instead. We'll learn more about the different pronoun options in the next section.

Questions You Might Be Afraid to Ask: Isn't Using *They* to Refer to One Person Grammatically Incorrect?

You might be surprised to learn that *they* as a singular pronoun has a long history. It's been used since the 14th century, and by some of the most famous English writers in history, like Jane Austen and William Shakespeare. For example:

There's not a man I meet but doth salute me
As if I were their well-acquainted friend
                              Shakespeare, A Comedy of Errors

It was only in the 19th century that grammarians began to advise writers against the singular *they* and to recommend the use of *he/him* pronouns to refer to an unknown person, as in "Every patron must return *his* books to the library." In fact, according to these writers, today's *he or she* would actually be incorrect, as *he* was thought to encompass both genders.

Why? For the same reason your English teacher used to tell you not to use contractions like *don't* or *can't* in formal writing, or not to end a sentence with a preposition: If you're in a position of authority, you can kind of just make up rules, even if they don't make the language easier to understand or reflect how real people speak and write.

Luckily, writers past and present have largely ignored these made-up rules, and the singular *they* has flourished. And even if your brain finds it hard to unlearn the rules against the singular *they*, you can at least appreciate that it's made it easier for people outside the gender binary to express themselves accurately.

Language isn't doing its job if it doesn't help people communicate. Gendered language doesn't always work, so the English-speaking world has made adjustments, like using *flight*

$\longrightarrow$

attendant instead of *stewardess*. It would be a shame to go back to the days of calling gay people *sodomites* or people with learning disabilities *backwards* out of loyalty to long-dead 19th-century sticklers.

Commonly Used Pronouns

Now we get to the nitty-gritty details of pronouns, gendered and gender neutral. It might be the first time you've thought about the parts of speech since you had to diagram sentences in high school. It's totally normal to struggle with gender-neutral pronouns at first, just like you might struggle to learn a second language. You don't have to be a grammar wizard to figure out how to use these pronouns smoothly and confidently—just use the example sentences below to practice. (We'll go over this in the table that follows, but for now, know that "xe"/"xem"/"xyr" are pronounced as if the "x" was a "z," and sound like *zee, zem, zeer*. "Hir" sounds like the word *here*.)

Subject: *He* threw the ball. *Xe* caught it.

Object: The pitcher threw the ball to *them*. They threw the ball to *her*. Then she threw the ball to *xem*.

Possessive determiner: This is *xyr* ball. That is *her* bat. And that is *hir* catcher's mitt.

Possessive pronoun: That catcher's mitt is *hirs*. That ball is *xyrs*. The catcher's mitt is *hers*.

Reflexive: He didn't want to pitch the game *himself*. So xe appointed *xyrself* the pitcher.

When people tell you their pronouns, they might say something like, "I use she/her pronouns." But you might also encounter someone who says "I use she/they," or "I use they/xe." This usually means that either set of pronouns is okay. If you're unsure, you can always say, "Do you have a preference for which ones I should use?"

Some of these pronouns might come easier to you than others. Since the plural they/them is a typical part of speech, it may be much easier to adjust to using these pronouns for a single person that it would be to start using sie/hir pronouns for that person. However, gender-neutral pronouns aren't necessarily interchangeable. Many people would find it uncomfortable if you were to use the wrong gender-neutral pronouns (or any pronouns when they asked for no pronouns), much as it might be uncomfortable for you if you were called "she" if you go by "he."

Remember that pronouns may not always agree with what you think someone of that gender "should" use. You might meet a binary male who uses gender-neutral pronouns, for example, or a nonbinary person who uses "she/her." For this reason, it's a good idea to say "she/her pronouns" or "he/him pronouns" rather than "male pronouns" or "female pronouns," since you don't have to be any particular gender to use these pronouns.

See pages 44–45 for a table of some of the most common pronouns.

	SUBJECT	OBJECT	POSSESSIVE DETERMINER
she/her	she	her	her
he/him	he	him	his
they/them	they	them	their
ze/zir, zie/zir	ze *or* zie (pronounced "zee")	zir (pronounced "zeer")	zir (pronounced "zeer")
ze/hir, zie/hir, sie/hir	ze *or* zie (pronounced "zee") or sie (pronounced "see")	hir (pronounced "here")	hir (pronounced "here")
xe/xem, xie/xem	xe *or* xie (pronounced "zee")	xem (pronounced "zem")	xyr (pronounced "zeer")
ey/em, e/em	ey (rhymes with "they") *or* e (pronounced "ee")	em	eir (rhymes with "their")
No pronouns	Use the person's name instead (e.g., "Nancy")	Nancy	Nancy's

POSSESSIVE PRONOUN	REFLEXIVE
hers	herself
his	himself
theirs	themself *or* themselves
zirs (pronounced "zeers")	zirself (pronounced "zeerself")
hirs (pronounced "here")	hirself (pronounced "here-self")
xyrs (pronounced "zeers")	xyrself (pronounced "xyrself")
eirs (rhymes with "theirs")	eirself (rhymes with "their self")
Nancy's	Nancy's self (can also change your phrasing—if you'd say "He went by himself" for someone who uses he/him pronouns, you could say "Nancy went alone")

Questions You Might Be Afraid to Ask: What Do You Do if You Accidentally Misgender Someone?

So you used your kid's old name, or you called your kid's friend Zach "she" instead of "they." What should you do in the moment when it happens?

When you notice you've made a mistake, correct yourself quickly and move on. Don't assume the person you're referring to didn't notice. But there's also no need to apologize—just say "I mean, Kathy," for instance, and move on. Apologizing excessively might make the other person uncomfortable, or make them feel like they have to take care of your emotions around their pronouns. Don't put undue emphasis on the correction, as you don't want to come across as patronizing. Just make it easy and seamless.

If you slip up repeatedly, you might want to talk to the other person later in a private place and apologize. This is true even if (especially if!) that person is your child. Tell them you're going to make an effort to do better in the future. Keep it short, and try not to sound defensive (e.g., "I'm trying"), or self-justifying, like "You've always been Bryan, and I've only known you as 'he,' so it's hard"—in fact, there's no reason to refer to the person's old name or pronouns at all when you apologize!

Some people are so afraid of slipping up that they decide not to use pronouns for certain people at all, even if they know that person's pronouns. It is not an ideal solution. Naturally, people will notice and feel singled out if you do so, especially if you're doing it for just one person.

Instead, practice using these pronouns privately so you're less likely to slip. See page 47 ("How to Get Comfortable Using New Terminology") for tips on how to practice.

Parenting Tips and Conversation Starters: How to Get Comfortable Using New Terminology

Okay, you know your teen's new name or new pronouns—now what? You probably won't internalize them overnight. But there are more ways to practice your teen's name and pronouns than just sitting around waiting for it to happen. Don't wait until your teen starts getting impatient! Here are some ways you can start getting comfortable using your teen's and other trans people's name and pronouns, and around gender-neutral language in general.

- If you're having trouble with gender-neutral pronouns like "they" or "zie," privately practice using them on a pet, an inanimate object, or a TV character. "The cartel is after Walter White—I wonder what they'll do to get out of this one." "No, don't throw the remote! Hand zim to me."

- Start using the singular "they" to refer to unknown people. If a plumber's on the way, say, "I don't know when they'll get here, but they'd better hurry!"

- Make up a story about the person whose name or pronouns you're having trouble remembering, or talk out loud about things you've done together. "*Tina* and I went to the mall so I could get *her* new school clothes, and *she* ended up buying a new backpack."

- Practice using gender-neutral language at work or with friends and family. Instead of saying "ladies and gentlemen" in a formal setting, say "folks," friends," "guests," or "everyone." Instead of saying "Hey, guys" or "Hi, ladies" in a casual setting, try saying "Hi, folks" or "Hey, y'all!" This is a good idea, anyway—you don't know who else might appreciate being included, even if you don't know for sure that someone in the group uses gender-neutral language for themself.

- In group settings like your book club or a PTA meeting, offer your own pronouns when you introduce yourself ("Hi, I'm Bill. My pronouns are he/him/his"). You might feel uncomfortable if you don't normally do this. That's a good thing! Practicing might help you internally normalize the idea that people's pronouns don't necessarily match gender stereotypes. And encouraging people to specify their pronouns by stating your own pronouns (while also giving people the space not to specify their own if they so choose) is a good idea anyway.

- Some people use pins or patches with their pronouns to help people remember. If your teen wants to go this route, help them pick some out.

What's in a Name? (A Lot, Actually)

It's common for a trans person to choose a different, more gender-affirming name when they come out. This presents an easy opportunity for you to celebrate and affirm their gender exploration. As we discussed in the last chapter, using your teen's new name could very well be the thing they appreciate most among the many ways you support them.

Your teen might end up trying out more than one name. Many teens find it safer or more comfortable to go by a more gender-neutral name or a shortened version of their birth name at first before deciding on a different name. And some teens go through several names before they pick one that suits them. As confusing as it might be to have to say "Elsa—no, Alma—no, I mean Helga," try not to show frustration or make your teen feel like they have to settle on something that doesn't fit them.

Using a different name for your teen might bring up some complicated emotions for you. You might have picked that name after weeks of trying to find the perfect one. Maybe your teen's old name holds the memory of a beloved relative or an important moment in your life. Remember that your teen's new name is sure to hold a special meaning to them in the same way that their old name was meaningful to you—in fact, one supportive thing you can do is ask them about that meaning. Remember it's okay to grieve your teen's old name and to seek support for this grief from other adults.

In this section, we'll talk a little bit more about what a name change might look like in practice, how you can support and advocate for your teen in this process.

Changing Names Officially and Unofficially

If your teen decides to use a new name, it might take some help on your part. The process of changing one's name can be a deeply validating milestone for many trans teens, and navigating these steps with your teen can be an opportunity to show how much you care.

Your teen may decide that they'd like to get a legal name or gender marker change. These two things can often be done at the same time. In the U.S., it usually means filing forms with several different government agencies:

- Go to your local *civil court* to file a petition for a name or gender marker change (which usually needs to be done before anything else).

- The *vital records department* in the state or city where your teen was born is where to change the name or gender marker on their birth certificate.

- If your teen has a driver's license or non-driver ID, go to your local *department of motor vehicles* to change their photograph, name, or gender marker.

- Head to your local *Social Security office* to change their name or gender marker on their Social Security record.

- If your teen has a passport, your local *passport agency* or passport service provider (which can sometimes be a post office or library) is where you change their passport photograph, name, or gender marker.

Your teen will probably also want to change their name with non-government organizations, like their school, bank, and health-care providers. You might want to help them make a list so they can keep track of who knows them by what name.

If your teen is unable to get a court order for a name change, or doesn't want to, that doesn't mean they have to keep going by their old name. In some states and cities, it's possible to change the name on your DMV ID without getting a court order. Many places have legal protections for people who would like to go by a name other than their legal name at school or work. And even where these laws don't exist, schools and workplaces are often willing to accommodate trans students anyway. (There's more information on official name changes in the Resources section on page 126.)

Unofficially, your teen may want to start going by a different name with family and friends. You'll need to have a conversation about whom to tell, when to tell them, and who'll do the telling. And you may need to come up with a plan for what happens if someone in the family isn't on board with your teen's new name or pronouns. Does your teen need you to correct people? Have a private conversation with grumpy Uncle Dave? Allow them to leave a family gathering if they're being misgendered? Listen to them and come up with a plan to respond based on their needs.

Questions You Might Be Afraid to Ask: What Does *Deadnaming* Mean?

Some trans people use the word *deadname* to refer to the name they were given at birth that they no longer use. *Dead-naming* is when you call someone by their old name after they've started going by a new name. You should avoid dead-naming your teen if they've asked you to use a new name for them.

If you slip up, do the same thing you'd do if you used the wrong pronoun. Correct yourself quickly and move on, apologize if you keep doing it, and resolve to practice so you get it right in the future.

Your teen may not always want you to use their new name. There might be times when your teen hasn't come out to certain people and they'd like you to refer to them by their old name for safety or privacy reasons. It's a good reason to have this conversation before that happens! But if your teen is out to someone as their new name, it's important to use this new name to that person, even out of your teen's earshot. You don't want that person to deadname your teen or get confused about what name to use.

This habit doesn't just apply to your teen's old name. It may be true of other aspects of your teen's life before they were able to express their gender. Your teen might be distressed to see old photos of themself in your house, or to hear you say, "When you were a little boy . . ."

This is another important conversation to have with your teen. How would they like you to handle these things? Change the way you talk about their past self? Refrain from mentioning that they were junior prom queen or an Eagle Scout? It's possible that even topics that seem harmless to you might cause your teen discomfort. It's another opportunity to show your teen that you're curious about their experiences and care about their comfort and happiness.

Parenting Tips and Conversation Starters: Getting Used to Your Teen's Identity

Still struggling? Sometimes, just knowing more about your teen's identity might make it easier to affirm and support them. Supporting them will be much easier if you know more about *why* they need that support and what it means to them. Here are some homework assignments to help you immerse yourself in your teen's world:

- Who shares your teen's identity? What are their lives like? Find an article, a poem, a social media story, or a memoir by a young person who uses the same identity label your teen uses, or who shares some of their experiences. If your teen is open to it, have a conversation about how their experiences have been similar to or different from that person's.

- How would your teen like you—and the world—to see them? Talk to your teen about what they'd like you to see in them, affirm about them, or understand about them.

- What gender-related conflicts or struggles has your teen experienced? It might be easier for your teen to talk about the ways other people have invalidated or discouraged them rather than the ways *you* might have inadvertently done so. Take note as you listen of how you might do better, and try to put yourself in your teen's place.

- What brings your teen joy? Seeing themself in a mirror wearing their favorite outfit? Hearing people use their new name? Being around other people who share their experiences? Talk to your teen about joyful, happy gender experiences they've had.

Key Takeaways

In this chapter, we covered ways you can affirm your teen's gender identity through language. Remember:

- Learning the basic terms to describe gender identity can go a long way in affirming and supporting your teen.

- You don't have to know exactly what your teen is experiencing to affirm their gender.

- Gender identity isn't the same as sexual orientation, and trans people can have any sexual orientation that cis people can.

- Gender *identity* is the inner stuff, and gender *expression* is the outward stuff.

- Validating language can help you talk about gender identity and expression with your teen with less friction.

- Gender-neutral language, including gender-neutral pronouns, can be useful—both in describing people whose gender is unknown or unimportant and in talking about someone who doesn't use gendered pronouns or language to describe themself.

- Your teen might want to change their name and gender marker, which can be done both officially (e.g., through a court order) or unofficially (e.g., telling friends and family). If your teen wants to do so, let them lead the way when it comes to how and when it happens.

In the next chapter, we'll talk about how you might be able to meet your teen's gender needs beyond language. We'll discuss how clothes, hair, and other aspects of gender expression can be used for affirmation, experimentation, and fun. And we'll talk about what your role is in helping and guiding your child through these changes—and the ways you can let your child guide you.

CHAPTER 3

Not Just Clothes

This chapter is all about the nuts and bolts of gender expression: clothes, hair, makeup, and personal grooming. When your teen decides to take steps to affirm their gender, clothes are probably the first stop. We'll talk about what to expect when your teen wants to experiment with their gender presentation and how to talk to your teen in a respectful, affirming manner.

The way your teen dresses and presents themself is about more than just signaling their gender to other people. Your teen is coming into a sense of who they are and how they'd like the world to see them—and not just when it comes to their gender. These years are also a time when people experiment with their identity in a more general way: figuring out the finer details of who they are and how they'd like others to see them.

In this chapter, we'll look at some of the reasons it might be important for your teen to express themself with their clothing or grooming choices. We'll talk about ways to help your teen navigate these steps, and we'll also take a look at gender-affirming accessories and undergarments that might help your teen feel more confident. Finally, we'll discuss ways of talking about this stuff with your teen that won't cause friction in your relationship.

Why Affirming Fashion Matters

One of the first things your teen might want to start doing as they explore their gender is change their clothing and style. You might wonder why it's so important to your teen to wear clothes that affirm their gender, or to experiment with different looks. *Didn't you say gender identity was more of an "inside your head" thing than an "outward self-expression" thing?*

It's true that our inner gender identity is separate from the outward ways we express our gender, like clothing. But that doesn't mean clothing doesn't reflect anything about your teen's identity. Clothing also serves as a shortcut to inform other people about how you'd like them to see you—gender included. And gender-affirming clothing might be more important to a trans teen than to a cis teen. A trans teen may not be able to take it for granted that others will affirm their gender if they're not wearing clothing that communicates it.

Clothing can also help your teen get more comfortable with their physical body. Many clothes and undergarments are designed to accentuate some parts of the body or de-emphasize others. The right outfit or haircut may reduce gender dysphoria and enable your teen to be confident enough to do things they wouldn't otherwise do.

What does any of this have to do with you? If your teen is already independently choosing and buying their clothes, you might wonder whether you have to do anything at all. However, helping your teen figure out their wardrobe might present another opportunity for you and your teen to build a stronger alliance.

For example, you may need to be an advocate for your teen at school if your teen's gender expression clashes with the dress code. Or you might need to help your teen purchase gender-affirming undergarments to help them get more comfortable with their body. You might also find yourself sharing the wisdom you've developed over the years, like how to tie a

Windsor knot or alter a blouse. Developing your teen's trust in you by helping them with gender-affirming clothing may signal that they can also come to you with higher-stakes concerns.

Most important, your role is to pay attention to what your teen is telling you they need. They might ask you to take them into the bra section and help them pick something out—or to wait patiently outside the store. You might be called on to tell them which shirt looks best with their favorite jacket—or to hold off on giving your opinion at all. There's no blanket rule for how to parent when it comes to clothing choices. The only rule is to listen.

Every request your teen makes of you is an opportunity to demonstrate that you're interested in their experiences and willing to hear them out. You'll also have many opportunities to set aside your own discomforts and fears in order to put your child's needs first. That's why clothing isn't *just* clothing. It's a tangible way to say to your child, "I see you the way you want me to see you, and I'd like other people to see you that way, too." This section will tell you how you can do so in concrete, practical ways.

Dealing with Fashion's Binary Problem

Unfortunately—outside trendy, expensive boutiques and gender-neutral specialty stores—most clothing stores are separated into men's and women's sections. This means teens looking for gender-neutral clothing options don't have a lot of . . . well, options. And even if your teen wants gendered clothing, the stuff they want might not fit them. It's tough to find men's chinos that look good on someone with larger hips, for example, or women's clothing with long enough sleeves for a tall person.

Alterations might work to get your teen's clothing looking the way they'd like it to. An inch added to a pant leg or subtracted from a sleeve may make for a perfect fit. If a professional tailor is too expensive, or your teen isn't comfortable getting measured, you or your teen might find it easier and cheaper to do it yourself. The Resources section on page 126 lists some places where you can learn how to perform simple alterations.

Many gendered items of clothing—like swimwear, activewear, and underwear—feature body-hugging styles that aren't comfortable for everyone. And many mainstream clothing stores don't include everyone's body in their sizing. A number of trans designers and specialty clothes companies have worked to solve these problems by creating clothing with less gendered styles, more inclusive sizes, and better fits for gender-variant bodies. If your teen struggles to find a swimsuit that doesn't scream "boy" or "girl," or button-up shirts cut for a bigger chest, these brands might provide much-needed affirmation. In the Resources section (page 126), you can learn more about buying clothes from these designers and companies.

Mainstream clothing brands and stores sometimes offer inclusive changing rooms and extended sizing that may make for a better shopping experience for your teen. Some stores have more accommodations than others. The Resources section (page 126) lists some of these stores and what they offer.

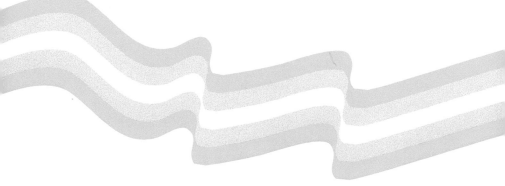

Questions You Might Be Afraid to Ask: If My Teen Prefers to Wear Clothes of a Different Gender, Does That Mean They're Trans?

Nope! Lots of teens wear clothing and accessories that aren't the norm for their assigned gender—for comfort, for self-expression, for experimentation, or just because they like how it looks. Maybe you remember trying out eyeliner during your Siouxsie and the Banshees phase, or buying a pair of pants from the men's section after failing to find anything with pockets in the women's. There's no reason your teen can't be the same, whatever their gender.

Remember that gender *expression* is different from gender *identity*. Although clothes can reflect gender identity, they don't have to rigidly adhere to gender boundaries. And the clothes we consider "men's" and "women's" have been drastically different throughout different time periods and in different places, from the elaborate wigs of fashionable European men in the Elizabethan era to the gender-bending women's outfits of the 1970s. You don't suddenly become a different gender because you put on a different outfit, or because trends have changed.

You can make your home a safe place for your teen to wear the clothes they like to wear without assuming that their clothing choice means anything in particular about their gender identity. You can also express a positive attitude toward trans identities, and welcome the possibility that your child *could* be trans, while letting them define who they are and not pushing them to adopt a label that doesn't fit them. Refusing to reinforce gender stereotypes makes your home a happier place for *any* teen, regardless of whether they're trans.

Parenting Tips and Conversation Starters: Decatastrophizing Your Shopping Trips

At some point, it's inevitable that you'll have one or two things to say about your kid's clothing choices. A lot of questions might pass through your mind while you wait endlessly in the changing room while your teen tries on yet another pair of jorts: *Is this outfit too weird? Too revealing? Will they get flak from their teachers? Get bullied? What will the neighbors say?*

It's also possible that your own emotions might get in the way of allowing your teen choices about how to dress. Your teen's clothing choices might clash with the image you have of them. Fears about bullying and discrimination might spring to mind no matter how supportive you are.

One technique that might help you put things in perspective is *decatastrophizing*. Decatastrophizing is a cognitive technique designed to ease anxiety by helping you put your worries in the larger context of your life and your teen's. Ask yourself:

- What's the absolute worst thing that could happen if your teen wore what they'd like to wear?

- How likely is this scenario to actually happen?

- If it *did* happen, what skills does your teen have that would help them get through it?

- What are the consequences of *not* letting your teen make this decision themself?

The teenage years present the perfect time to take risks. A teenager has both the brainpower to make their own decisions and the support of caring adults to fall back on when things get tough. In fact, teenagers *need* to take risks in order to learn the skills of adulthood.

Courage and self-confidence don't develop automatically. Teens need to experience the process of coming to decisions and navigating the consequences of those decisions. Teens who aren't allowed to make important decisions—the kind that have actual consequences, good or bad—can have trouble making decisions when they become adults, and might experience anxiety and indecision over even relatively safe choices.

Compared to many situations your teen will encounter in life—*Drugs! Sex! Burning Man!*—choosing what to wear is a relatively safe training ground for decision-making. Not only will your teen get a confidence boost from your trust in them, but the relationship will also improve when your teen sees that you respect their judgment and autonomy, even when you disagree with their decisions.

So let's say you're tempted to say something like *Grandma's going to freak out if you show up with blue hair,* or *Could you maybe dial back the tightness of those pants?* When it happens, walk yourself through some of those questions. It might also help to think about the skills you developed when your parents let you express yourself and develop a sense of independence. Did *you* drop dead on the spot when someone made fun of your short-lived mullet, or when you got sent to the principal's office for wearing a skirt that was *juuuust* a bit too short? If you're reading this, probably not. Instead, it's likely that you learned a little about decision-making and risk-taking without even realizing it. Let your teen have the same experience.

Beyond Skirts and Suits: A Guide to Gender-Affirming Undergarments and Accessories

Many trans teens choose to wear accessories and undergarments that shape or augment their bodies in ways that make them more comfortable. Your teen might want to make their chest look bigger or smaller, for example, or emphasize or de-emphasize their hips. These garments can be found in specialty stores for trans people, often online. They can also be DIY'd from other easy-to-find types of clothing, like underwear and sports bras.

Parents of trans teens often have a lot of questions about these garments. *Are these products safe? Are there any long-term effects? Do I have to go to a shady store by the highway to buy them? Can they be mail-ordered in a plain, discreet box like that thigh cream I bought last summer?* We'll answer all these questions and more in this section.

Here are some of the most common gender-affirming undergarments and accessories your teen might need:

For teens assigned female at birth:

- A *binder* is a piece of clothing designed to make your teen's chest look flatter. It typically looks like a sports bra or an undershirt. Usually, it goes under whatever your teen is wearing, although some can be worn alone like a tank top or shirt. There are also special types of *tape* that can be used to safely make one's chest look smaller.

- Some transmasculine people wear *compression garments* to de-emphasize the appearance of their hips and buttocks. These are sometimes labeled with words like *shaping, sculpting, slimming*, or *compression*. Many are designed for both cisgender and transgender men and sold in mainstream stores.

- A *packer* creates a bulge in a pair of pants or swimwear. Packers are usually made from silicone or some other soft, durable material. Your teen may wear one with a specially designed pair of underwear to help it stay in place. Some packers also function as *stand-to-pee devices*, which (as the name implies) allow a transmasculine person to pee standing up at a urinal or toilet.

- Some *period underwear* is made especially for transmasculine people who menstruate, such as boxers and briefs that make it easier to use a pad than traditional men's underwear do. Other types of period underwear are designed in masculine styles with a washable, reusable pad to catch menstrual blood.

For teens assigned male at birth:

- *Breast prosthetics* create the appearance of a larger chest. There are many different types for different needs. Some take the form of bras with built-in prosthetics, and other bras have pockets for inserts of various sizes (sometimes called a *pocket bra*). There are also breast forms, usually made of silicone or another soft material, that attach to the chest with adhesive. Transfeminine teens who already have some breast growth as a result of hormones may want bras with extra padding for a fuller look. Some of these items were originally designed for cis women who have had mastectomies and can be found in certain medical supply stores.

- Your teen might want to wear *shapewear* that creates the appearance of a smaller waist, or with padding in areas like the buttocks and hips. Many products are available in mainstream women's clothing stores, often with labels like *sculpting, shaping, control, smoothing,* or *lifting.*

- A *gaff* is a pair of underwear designed to hide a transfeminine person's genitals (a process some people call "tucking"). These can come in the form of special underwear, or garments that can be worn under regular underwear.

Where can you buy this stuff? In the Resources section on page 126, you'll find information about online specialty stores by and for trans people that offer gender-affirming garments in many price ranges. These stores are able to ship items in discreet packaging to protect your teen's privacy.

However, you might not have to go to a special store to get these garments. Many shapewear items can be found in mainstream women's clothing and lingerie stores, and some breast forms can be purchased at stores that primarily sell to cis women who have had mastectomies. Some sports stores sell men's compression underwear/shapewear that might work for a transmasculine teen. Sports bras can also make good binders—just make sure you follow the safety tips in the next section. (There are also binder and bra exchanges for low-income teens at many trans-focused health clinics. Look at the Resources section on page 126, or ask your local LGBTQ center for help.)

Using Gender-Affirming Undergarments and Accessories Safely

You might be wondering whether gender-affirming underwear and accessories are safe for your teen to use, or whether they are accompanied by any long-term negative effects. Some—like packers and breast prosthetics—pose no known risks to teens. Others, while largely considered safe, have some associated risks that can be mitigated with safe use.

Binding and binders come with a few easily avoided risks. Research suggests that binding too tightly can make your teen's back or chest hurt, restrict their breathing, or even lead to rib fractures. Your teen should make sure they can breathe comfortably and aren't experiencing pain, numbness, tingling, or lightheadedness. Binders should be washed regularly to prevent irritation and infections. Your teen should never use Ace bandages or duct tape, which can damage skin, constrict breathing, and cause rib fractures. Taking a day off, if practical, can reduce the risks of binding. Some people use specially designed tape to masculinize their chest by taping their breast tissue back toward the armpits, which is safer than binding. However, this tape should never be worn *around* the chest.

Although there's no research to suggest that shapewear for either transfeminine or transmasculine people can be harmful to health, it's likely that some of the risks of binding also apply to other types of shapewear that fit over your teen's torso or abdomen. The same rules apply: make sure your teen can breathe, that the shaping garment is washed regularly, and that they aren't experiencing pain or irritation.

Many transfeminine people use tucking, which is the practice of arranging and folding genitals to smooth their outward appearance. There are different ways to do so safely, including using a gaff, which is a tight undergarment designed to pull a transfeminine person's genitals downward. You can find places online that sell gaffs and other tucking underwear, and sites that can guide your teen in DIY-ing their own, in the Resources section (page 126).

Tucking can also be done with specially designed medical tape. Your teen should not use duct tape or any adhesive that is not designed to go on the body. But most important, tucking shouldn't hurt. If anything causes pain, your teen should adjust how tightly they're tucking or use a different method. There are no known risks to tucking, which means that if your teen isn't feeling any pain, they're probably okay. Look at the Resources section on page 126 for links to tucking tips.

Questions You Might Be Afraid to Ask: Why Is My Teen Changing Some Parts of Their Appearance But Not Others?

It's common for trans people to feel different about certain parts of their bodies or aspects of their appearance. Gender dysphoria and euphoria isn't uniform across all trans people. Your teen might feel different about their chest than their legs, for example, or place a higher priority on body hair than facial hair. Your teen might want to change a lot of things at once, or nothing at all.

Why? Think about the last time you went to the beach on a crowded day. You probably saw all kinds of bodies, and many of them likely didn't conform to social norms for men and women. Maybe you saw women with a bit more facial or body hair than others, or men with big hips and chests. Statistically, the vast majority of these people were probably cisgender. Some of these people might feel uncomfortable with their bodies and want to change or hide some parts of themselves. (Think about a time you might have bought a padded bra as a teenager, or worn a shirt in the pool.) But others might be completely comfortable and not want to do anything differently. Same with trans people! Everyone's feelings about their body and the way it meshes with traditional gender standards are different—trans or cis.

It's also possible that your teen needs to experiment with different ways of presenting themself before they get comfortable with a specific look. For some trans teens, experimentation is the only way to figure out exactly how they feel when they look a certain way. So don't be surprised if your teen changes up their look from week to week. As with any teen, it's all part of getting comfortable in their own skin.

Parenting Tips and Conversation Starters: Talking to Your Teen about Their Influences

Some of the things that pop out of your teen's mouth might surprise you. Perhaps you're asking, "Where'd they hear that? What is a 'thigh gap' and who told them they were supposed to have one?" Friends or the internet might have given them unrealistic ideas about what their body is supposed to look like, or misinformation about sexuality and health.

So how do you even broach these subjects? These conversation topics might give you a place to start.

- What does your teen believe about body shape and size? Talk to your teen about how they and their friends talk about bodies. Do they say *fat* like it's a bad word? Do they make fun of people who don't fit the social ideal? Pressure one another to change things about their bodies? Now's a good time to check in with your teen and encourage them to talk to you about how their friends make them feel. You might also want to talk about how trans bodies and other bodies that don't fit the norm are portrayed in the media they consume and the social media accounts they follow. Do TV shows and movies make them feel better or worse about their own bodies?

- What does your teen know about sexuality? There might be gaps in their knowledge that "the talk" didn't cover, and good info might be mixed in with half-truths and misunderstandings. Turn to page 79 ("Because Sex Happens") to learn about gender-inclusive sex education, or to the Resources section on page 126 to read more about sex education resources for trans teens.

- Where does your teen get their information about trans identity? For some teens, friends—online and in person—can be great resources for information about trans life. However, trans teens are just as susceptible to misinformation as anyone else. If your teen's friends seem to be saying things that invalidate, hurt, or confuse your teen, talk to your teen about where to find more information from trusted sources. The Resources section on page 126 has ... you guessed it ... resources!

- What information is your teen getting from the internet? For most trans teens, the internet is an important pit stop for information and community. But it might also be a place where your teen learns harmful untruths about trans identities, or meets people who manipulate or bully them. The internet can be tricky because your teen might worry that you'll restrict their access if they tell you they're having problems with people online. Make sure your teen knows that you're willing to respect their privacy and honor the fact that the internet is a valuable resource for them—while also letting them know that they can come to you if they're not feeling safe.

Personal Grooming for Trans Teens

Clothing isn't the only way your teen might want to affirm their gender. Hair, makeup, skincare, and grooming products can help your teen look and feel the way they need to. For many teens, just having access to gender-affirming products and experimenting with different ways of grooming themselves can make them feel happier and more secure, even if they haven't yet gone public with their identity.

Your teen likely needs more privacy during this time. They probably don't want to share every detail of their new grooming routine with you or the rest of the family. They might need a locking door on their bedroom or their own private drawer in the family's shared bathroom. If you've always bought them grooming products in the past, they might need you to let them pick their own instead.

It's also possible that your teen doesn't quite know what to do about their grooming routine. You might never have thought you'd have to teach your teen how to shave when you still saw them as your daughter. Your teen may not have anyone but you to teach them these skills, so be ready to help.

In this section, we'll talk about the ways your teen might want to affirm their gender with personal grooming. I'll answer some common questions parents have about trans teens and grooming, and we'll discuss ways to open up a dialogue with your teen about these topics in a sensitive, caring way.

To Shave or Not to Shave

Some parents are confused when trans kids don't conform to their identified gender's grooming standards, or don't seem to want to adhere to the traditional image of that gender. What if your trans daughter doesn't want to shave her legs, or your trans son loves his long hair? What if your nonbinary child doesn't make the kinds of changes you expect them to make—or you don't know *what* changes to expect them to make?

It should come as no surprise that a teenager might reject traditional grooming standards. You probably remember doing this when you were a teen: *Do I really have to wax my upper lip just because Great Aunt Aida said I needed to? Hall and Oates have bushy hair—why can't I? What's wrong with wearing Old Spice deodorant instead of Lady Speed Stick?* Like any teen, yours might decide they're okay going outside the grooming norms for their gender.

Remember, grooming standards aren't what validate or invalidate your gender identity, whether you're trans or cis. Your child's hair doesn't make them a different gender than they say they are any more than it does for famously shaggy Russell Brand or closely cropped Ginnifer Goodwin. And no one with any sense has ever said that a cis woman with unshaven legs has forfeited womanhood. Make sure you're not holding your trans teen to different standards than you do for people who aren't trans.

It's also true that many teens decide to take things slowly for their own comfort or safety. Maybe your teen isn't ready to field intrusive questions about why they've suddenly started changing their appearance, even if they might want to take bolder steps in the future when they're feeling safer. Or maybe your teen feels more comfortable showing off their new hairstyle or makeup routine in some settings, but not others.

So don't worry if your teen doesn't accept the razors, creams, clippers, and colognes that commercials push on them. As long as your teen is showering regularly and brushing their teeth, that's fine. Your role in your child's life doesn't need to be as an enforcer of gender norms. Your teen faces all kinds of pressure from the rest of the world, from the kind of clothes they should wear to the kind of music they should listen to. It doesn't help to add yourself to the army of people telling your teen what they "should" be doing.

Questions You Might Be Afraid to Ask: What Does *Passing* Mean?

Passing is a word that some trans people use to describe whether other people can tell if they're trans. If you pass, it means other people assume that you're a cisgender person of your identified gender. For some people, it can be highly affirming and come with a sense of gender euphoria. For others, it's important to their safety in public places.

Many people dislike the word *passing* because they feel that it implies they're tricking or deceiving other people. And some trans people feel that being visibly trans isn't something that needs to change about them. In fact, for many trans

$\longrightarrow$

people, being visibly trans is a positive—or they're not concerned how others see them at all. You should not assume your teen's goal is to blend in with cisgender people.

For some trans people, passing can be a double-edged sword. It's true that being accepted as one's identified gender without questions or comments can be affirming and safe. However, this can come with a fear of one's trans status being discovered. And many trans people *want* to be out to others and feel uncomfortable hiding that fact.

Your teen might feel the need hide their trans status in some settings, fearing discrimination or violence, or simply wanting to avoid uncomfortable questions and rude comments. Some people refer to secrecy around trans status as *going stealth* or *stealth mode*—as in, "I'm stealth at work, but I'm out at school."

You'll want to have a conversation with your teen about how you can support them in keeping their history private in certain settings if they choose to do so. Remember it's your teen's right to choose how to handle their personal information, and staying private about these things is neither deceptive nor dishonest. No teenager should be forced to give up personal or medical details to satisfy others' curiosity. Help them develop a simple response for prying questions, like "That's between my doctor and me."

Parenting Tips and Conversation Starters: Talking to Your Teen about Grooming

Learning about grooming and hygiene from your parents is an age-old rite of passage. What better way to affirm and/or embarrass your teen? Here are some ways you can have supportive, helpful conversations with your teen about grooming.

- **Help with Shaving, Styling, and Shopping.** For many teens—trans and cis—getting your help and advice on grooming can be an important rite of passage.

Share a moment with your teen by taking them out to buy grooming products that fit their gender, or for a gender-affirming haircut. If they're comfortable with your help, teach them a few tricks: how to shave their face or legs without cutting themself, or to get the perfect updo.

- **Understand Age Is Just a Number.** Some of the things your teen might want to do may strike you as age-inappropriate. Perhaps you're worried that your teen is too young for makeup or shapewear. Although it's okay to set boundaries with your teen, remember trans teens may have different considerations that might warrant an exception to your usual household rules. Your trans teen might struggle to express their gender to others or to feel comfortable in their bodies without the help of grooming or undergarments that might seem unnecessary to a cis teen—for whom puberty might have already done most of the work. Talk to your teen about what they're trying to achieve and try to understand how their needs might be different from a cis teen's.

- **Make an Offer.** Your teen might not know how you're willing to help them or what they can ask of you when it comes to clothing and grooming. Maybe they're not sure about *your* comfort level around these topics, especially if you haven't had many conversations like this. It's a good reason to be proactive instead of waiting for them to come to you. Let them know you're willing to go makeup shopping with them, make some adjustments to their clothes, or teach them to paint their nails.

- **Extend an Invitation.** If you arrange a spa day with the women in your family, but you don't invite your transfeminine teen to join, you might send the message that you don't take their gender seriously or see them in the same way you see other girls and women. Make sure your trans teen is included in any activity that's separated by gender. If in doubt, ask them. And ask yourself whether these activities *have* to be separated by gender. It's possible your transmasculine child doesn't want to stop going back-to-school shopping with their favorite aunt just because they don't identify as female. And your transfeminine child probably still wants help and advice from their dad.

Key Takeaways

As you reflect on all the ways you can help your teen develop a sense of themself by exploring their gender expression, keep in mind:

- Clothes and grooming can help your teen explore and express who they are and make them feel more comfortable in their body.

- Clothing can be tailored to your teen's body, and many fashion brands offer extended sizing and gender-neutral styles.

- Gender expression is different from gender identity, and wearing clothing of a particular style doesn't necessarily mean anything about your teen's identity.

- Gender-affirming undergarments and accessories—like shapewear and prosthetics—can help your teen express their gender and feel more at home in their skin.

- Many trans teens decide to change different parts of their appearance and not others.

- Your teen probably needs more privacy right now, such as a locking bedroom door or a separate drawer in the bathroom.

- Your teen's grooming routine might not conform to that of their identified or assigned gender. Your teen might also experiment with different grooming routines. All this is totally normal!

In the next chapter, we'll talk about some of the other ways trans teens might align their bodies with their self-image, such as gender-affirming medical procedures. We'll also talk about some other questions parents of trans teens might have about trans bodies, like how to talk about sexuality with your trans teen.

CHAPTER 4

Bodies and Bits: Understanding Your Teen's Body Needs

In this chapter, we're going to take a look at some things that might seem scary to you: surgery, hormones, health, and (gasp!) talking about sex with your teen. But I promise you'll feel less scared when you finish this chapter. The recommendations I make will be supported by research evidence, and I'll answer questions about common anxieties parents often have about trans teen bodies.

The topics we discuss in this chapter might make you or your teen uncomfortable. You might think, *I could never say this to my teen!* or *My kid would cover their ears if I tried to start a conversation about masturbation.* And maybe your teen isn't interested in hormones or surgery at this point, so you don't feel like you need to have that talk.

Those things might be 100 percent true, but laying a foundation of trust and communication now will encourage your teen to come to you when they have questions or need help. And having resources on hand to help your teen learn about their body and sexuality not only provides expert information beyond what you might be able to tell them but also helps you open up a dialogue by showing you recognize how important these issues are to them.

First, we'll talk about the sex ed topics your teen might need to know, especially those specific to trans and queer teens. We'll go over both physical stuff like STIs and pregnancy and emotional stuff like relationships, safety, and consent. Then we'll discuss some of the medical procedures that can help trans teens get their bodies in sync with their self-image. We'll also look at different ways of talking to your teen about these subjects that might cut through the awkwardness and dispel some of your anxieties.

Because Sex Happens: Going Beyond Traditional Sex Ed

When you were in high school, did you learn anything about transgender sexuality in your sexual education classes? No? Well, chances are, your teen hasn't either. Even if your teen's school has the latest, most up-to-date sex ed curriculum, it's likely that it included—at best—a mention of the existence of trans identities. And when you think back to "the talk" you may have had with your teen, you might now struggle to imagine how the lessons you taught about sex at the time apply to them now.

Why is it important for a trans teen to know about these things—especially if you don't think your teen is having sex? What good could come from the painful, cringeworthy conversation that neither of you wants to have?

First of all, it's important that your teen knows that being trans doesn't mean anything about their ability to have the kinds of relationships and sex they want in the future. Sex education that excludes trans sexuality can make trans teens feel excluded or "other." Your teen may feel stigmatized, confused, or left out of their peer group when classmates are talking about sex. Knowing about the ways trans people can have happy and fulfilling sex lives can right this wrong.

Second, trans teens may be more vulnerable to relationship violence, sexual harassment, and other abusive or unwanted contact. They may not be able to handle these experiences on their own, or even understand them. Talking to your teen about what to do about sexual and relationship violence can help them problem-solve when the time comes and build their trust in your willingness to help them if they're in crisis.

Third, and most important, there will come a time when your teen has to make their own decisions about sex and relationships. However cautious a parent you are, and however much you counsel your child about safety and good decision-making, and however smart and capable your child is, they'll be sure to make at least one or two not-so-smart decisions in the heat of the moment.

What happens afterward—whether they seek help, and how much they tell you about what's going on—will be determined by your relationship with them. If you've cultivated a relationship that allows for honesty and non-judgmental dialogue, your teen will be better equipped to weather these times and be open with you about their missteps.

Sometimes you'll be at a loss for words when your teen asks you questions about sexuality. Rest assured, you don't need to know everything. It's more helpful to direct your teen toward trusted sources of information than to try to answer questions you don't understand. Page 129 in the Resources section has information about where to find trans- and queer-affirming sex education resources online.

Safe Sex Is More Than Just Protection

Sexuality and relationships are about more than putting a condom on a banana in health class. Your teen needs to know about not just the practical aspects of sex, but also the emotional ones. And if your teen's knowledge of sex only extends to how babies are made (or how to prevent babies from being made), they might miss out on the joyful, positive aspects, especially if their body or identity doesn't fit the cisgender mold.

Here are some topics of conversation you might want to bring up with your teen. You should also let them know there are many resources available online and in print beyond what you're able to teach them. Your teen can learn all about these topics using the Resources section (page 126).

Does your teen know *how STIs are transmitted*? It's not the same with every STI, and your teen should know what types of activities put them at more or less risk. Your teen should also know that some activities present little to no risk of STI transmission—like only touching with hands, for example.

Does your teen know about *barrier methods* to prevent STIs? Make sure your teen is aware of external and internal condoms, gloves, and dental dams as effective methods of preventing STI transmission. Ensure that they know that using lubricant during sexual activity can help reduce STI risk by reducing friction that can cause skin to get irritated or tear or condoms to break. You might want to talk to your teen about the possibility of buying these items for them, or give them money to purchase them on their own. In some places, teens and adults can get free condoms and other sexual health products from their local health authority, clinic, or certain Planned Parenthood locations, and some are available by mail.

Does your teen know about *pre-exposure* and *post-exposure prophylaxis* (more commonly known as PrEP and PEP)? These medications can reduce the risk of contracting HIV. PrEP is a medication taken regularly by people at risk for HIV. When taken as prescribed, PrEP reduces the risk of getting HIV by about 99 percent. Your teen can talk to their primary care provider or local sexual health clinic to figure out whether they need PrEP. PEP is a medication given for a short period of time after a sexual encounter that may have put your teen at risk for contracting HIV. The sooner it's taken, the more effective it is. Your teen should know to visit a sexual health clinic, urgent care clinic, emergency room, or their primary care provider to obtain PEP, ideally within two hours after the sexual encounter (but as soon as possible after that).

Have you and your teen talked to their primary care pro-vider about the *Gardasil HPV vaccine*? Gardasil is approved for children and teens ages 9 and up and can prevent your teen from getting sexually transmitted strains of HPV. All teens should get this vaccine as soon as they're eligible to protect themselves against genital warts, anal warts, and cancer caused by HPV.

Does your teen know how to access *STI testing*? You might hope your teen never has an STI scare, but just in case, it might be helpful for them to know about sexual health clinics that can provide easy, accurate, private testing. Some schools even offer these services.

Does your teen know how to reduce the risk of pregnancy through *contraception* (also known as *birth control*)? Even if your teen is not sexually active—or you don't think they are—talk to your teen about the many different contraceptive methods available. You may also want to take them to a sexual health clinic like Planned Parenthood to speak with a health-care provider or sex educator.

Is your teen able to access *trans-affirming medical care*? Some trans teens purchase hormones from friends, off the internet, or from the street if they can't get them legally and safely. These substances may not be what they say on the label. And if your teen uses injectable hormones and shares a needle, they risk contracting HIV, hepatitis B and C, and other diseases. Talk to your teen about these risks and help them access health care that affirms their gender identity.

Can your teen navigate *consent*? Talk about asking for and giving permission—not just for sexual activities, but for things like touching, kissing, and other intimate contact. Make sure they know they don't owe someone sex just because they're in a relationship, and that consent violations can happen to anyone of any gender. Talk about the effect of pressure and coercion and how it might make someone feel like they have to say "yes" even when they'd rather say "no." Discuss alcohol and drugs and how they might impair someone's ability to consent.

Does your teen know about *sexuality beyond reproduction*? Many sex ed classes only teach about penis-in-vagina (PIV) sex between cisgender people. Needless to say, trans teens often struggle to imagine what partnered or solo sex might look like for them, or wonder whether they'll find someone who wants to have the kind of sex they want to have. They'll likely want to know the finer details about how trans people have sex, or how they can masturbate in a way that makes them feel at home in their body. It's okay if you feel out of your depth talking about these subjects. The Resources section (page 126) has some teen-friendly sites that can help your teen learn how sexuality works for trans people.

Does your teen know what to do if they experience *relationship violence*? Physical and emotional abuse in romantic relationships is more common among LGBTQ youth, although the reasons are unclear. Have a conversation about physical and emotional abuse with your teen and talk about what to do if they feel unsafe in a relationship, or if they're sexually harassed.

You'll also want to talk about *online sexual abuse and harassment*, which is also higher among LGBTQ teens. Talk to your teen about what to do if someone sends them unwanted sexual photos or messages, pressures them into sending their own photos, sends their photos to others without permission, threatens to out them as trans to other people, or makes harassing social media posts about them. Make sure your teen knows you won't get mad or punish them if they tell you they've sent sexual photos or messages to someone, looked at adult websites, or posted images of themself online.

Can your teen *talk to you and other trusted adults* about sex and relationships? I've worked with many teens whose parents wouldn't hesitate to answer "yes" to that question. Those same teens would come into my office every week and tell me how impossible it was to talk to their parents about sex.

Some teens sense that their parents are anxious or overwhelmed by these topics and decide to avoid the awkwardness of these conversations altogether. Others know their parents might get angry or restrict their privileges if they knew they were having sex or dating someone. Still others worry that their parents will intervene or give unwanted or unhelpful advice. Trans teens especially worry that their parents won't even understand what they're talking about, let alone be able to help or comfort them.

There's no easy way to deal with these issues. If your teen doesn't feel like they can talk to you about sex, it doesn't mean you've *intentionally* caused them to feel this way. However, you can still work to change the situation. This will involve more than a single conversation. It will mean graciously accepting feedback from your teen when you make a mistake. You may need to do some reading and research to get yourself up to speed on topics that are important to your teen. It might mean changing the way you talk about sex in your household, or thinking about how your household rules and messaging around sex might encourage your teen to keep secrets from you. Or it may mean owning up to things you've said in the past that might have sent the wrong message to your teen.

Above all, solving this problem means listening without judgment when your teen tells you something important. Turn to page 86 ("How to Use Active Listening to Talk to Your Teen about Sex") for more info on how to start.

Questions You Might Be Afraid to Ask: Is My Trans Teen More At Risk for STIs Than Other Teens?

Not necessarily. When we talk about the risk of HIV and other STIs, we often hear it framed in terms of sexual orientation or gender identity. You might hear people say things like, "Gay people are more likely to get STIs than straight people" or "HIV is common in the trans community." The problem with this framing is that STI risk is about *sexual behavior* and *sexual networks*, not about who you are or whom you're attracted to.

What does this mean? *Sexual behavior* refers to the way you have sex. It's not just what kind of sex you're having or how many partners you have, but also whether you use condoms or other barriers, ask sexual partners to test themselves for STIs, test regularly yourself, take medications like PrEP for HIV prevention, or use other safer sex methods. (With some STIs, certain non-sexual behaviors also matter—for example, injectable drug users who share needles are at high risk for HIV and hepatitis B and C, as are trans people who share needles to inject hormones.)

Sexual network refers to who you have sex with. It also includes the people *those* people are having sex with. Your sexual partners can increase or decrease your STI risk depending on the STI risk of the *other* people they're having sex with, the number of partners they have, the types of sex they have with those people, the safer sex methods they're using, and other activities like drug use.

Sexual behavior and sexual networks greatly affect STI risk. Some types of sex are riskier than others, and using safer sex methods can greatly reduce or eliminate these risks. And some sexual networks present higher risk for STIs.

However, although sexual networks and sexual behavior do affect STI transmission, your teen shouldn't rely on their perception of how "safe" or "risky" a given partner's sexual network might seem. Instead, they should know about how to make sex safer with *every* partner.

What does this mean for you? When you talk about safer sex with your teen, it's important to focus on behavior rather than identity. If they're not having sex, their identity does not put them at increased risk for STIs, period. And if they *are* having sex, their identity isn't a modifiable factor, and they can't just change their gender identity or sexual orientation to reduce their STI risk. What they can do—and what you can help them do—is learn about ways of making sex safer regardless of what partners they choose.

Why am I saying "safer" instead of "safe"? Because sex is inherently risky. We accept these risks because we feel that sexual relationships are worth it. You've likely accepted a certain amount of sexual risk into your life. Your teen will, too—but that doesn't mean you can't help them lower those risks.

Parenting Tips and Conversation Starters: How to Use Active Listening to Talk to Your Teen about Sex and Relationships

Active listening is a useful skill when you're parenting a trans teen. Young people often tell me that the most supportive thing their parents do is listen without judgment, even if their parents can't fix the problem or offer useful advice. This is especially true when it comes to sensitive topics like sex and romantic relationships. One of the easiest ways to improve your relationship with your teen—another "free space" of parenting—is to listen actively and attentively.

We're not trained to be active listeners from birth, and our deeply ingrained conversational habits often get in the way. Parents who can listen to their teen say things that confuse them, annoy them, anger them, or make them feel inadequate—all without passing judgment or trying to fix the problem—are something akin to superhuman.

Being an active listener about sex probably won't come naturally to you. That's okay! It doesn't come easily to most people, and it's a skill that involves suppressing a lot of your natural impulses. You won't always get it right. For instance, when your teen is telling you about last night's argument with their Exhausting Boyfriend Aiden, you might feel the urge to do any number of these things:

- Give advice
- Defend yourself if you feel criticized
- Express moral judgment
- Blame your teen for what's happening
- Express discomfort
- Change the subject
- Fill the silence

- Get distracted by household tasks

- Interrupt (even if it's to ask a question)

- Offer solutions or try to fix things

- Get angry on your teen's behalf

- Express doubt about your teen's perspective

- Get frustrated that your teen won't get to the point

- Argue with an opinion your teen expressed

Try to recognize this behavior and stop yourself when you're giving in to any of these urges. Instead, try some of these active listening strategies:

- Give your teen your full attention. If you're really busy, set aside a time later in the day to talk, and keep your promise. Don't get caught up in other household problems or let other people interrupt. Your teen will appreciate that you're prioritizing them over distractions.

- Think about your facial expressions and tone of voice. Make your posture as open as possible. Your teen knows you well enough that they can probably guess when you're receptive to what they're saying. It's okay not to completely be able to control your facial expressions, but try to temper any obvious looks of discomfort.

- Ask open-ended questions, such as, "What do you plan to do about it?" These kinds of questions are usually better at keeping your teen talking openly with you than yes-or-no questions like, "Are you going to break up with Jo?"

- Talk about feelings, not just hard facts. Reflect and label emotions if you can. You can say things like, "So when Dana kissed you, it was the happiest you've felt all week?" If you're not sure what your teen was feeling, you also can ask an open-ended question: "How did you feel when that happened?"

- Ask for clarification when you need to. There's no shame in admitting when you don't understand exactly what your teen is saying or why it's important. Don't judge or ridicule them for talking about something that doesn't make sense to you, even if what they're worried about sounds silly or inconsequential. It's okay to say something like, "I know this is important to you, and I'm going to try my best to understand."

- Try not to make it about you. Your teen's relationship problems aren't a referendum on your parenting skills. And if your teen rejects your advice, it doesn't mean it was bad advice. Celebrate the fact that your teen is exercising their independence and autonomy, and don't mourn the fact that their brain isn't in lockstep with yours.

Understanding Gender-Affirming Hormone Therapy (GAHT)

Gender-affirming hormone therapy is a term used to describe medical treatments that introduce hormones into a trans person's body in order to help align it with their gender identity. You might have also heard it described as *hormone replacement therapy (HRT)*, and some trans teens call these treatments "T" or "E," which are short for testosterone and estrogen. Hormonal treatments for gender affirmation also include *puberty suppression*, more commonly referred to as *puberty blockers*, which halt some of the effects of puberty in trans youth. Trans teens who use these treatments experience not only less gender dysphoria, but also better functioning, well-being, and quality of life.

Teens under the age of 18 will need a letter from a psychotherapist or other mental health-care professional specializing in gender identity to access hormone therapy. This therapist may see your teen for a limited time to collaboratively assess whether hormone therapy is right for them. Or your teen might want to see a therapist for a longer period for ongoing therapy. As part of the process of writing a letter of support, the therapist will talk to you and your family and answer any questions you might have about why hormone therapy might be indicated.

If the therapist decides to write a letter of support for hormone therapy, your teen will need an endocrinologist or trans-competent primary care provider to provide a prescription and educate you and your teen about its effects. This provider will order blood tests and assess your teen's overall health, and will counsel you and your teen about the risks and benefits of treatment. They will follow up with your teen regularly to monitor your teen's hormone levels and other health indicators. You can find information about trans-competent therapists, doctors, and other professionals in the Resources section (page 126).

Not all trans teens want hormone therapy, and not all trans people take hormones for their entire lives. Some trans people decide to undergo hormone therapy for a short period of time to achieve the effects they're looking for and then stop when they're satisfied. Others stop hormone therapy for other reasons, such as childbearing. And some trans people don't want hormone therapy at all. It's a personal decision for your teen to make based on their feelings about their body. A trans-competent therapist and primary care provider can help them make an informed decision.

Many parents wonder whether gender-affirming hormone therapy has any negative effects. Luckily, hormone therapy has been administered to trans people for decades, and scientific research on this topic has a long history. Research suggests hormone therapy in trans people is largely safe and its small increased health risks in some populations can be addressed with monitoring by health professionals. It's an important topic to bring up with your teen's endocrinologist or primary care provider if you have concerns.

All about Testosterone

Testosterone is usually prescribed in injectable form, and your teen may need to learn to self-inject. It can also be prescribed in the form of a gel, an implant, or a patch. The most common effects of testosterone are a deeper voice, darker and thicker facial and body hair, increase in skin thickness, redistribution of fat deposits on the body and face, clitoral growth, halting of menstrual periods, and increased muscle mass. When your teen becomes an adult, testosterone could also lead to thinning hair, although there are medications to address this.

Some people who use testosterone also develop oily skin or acne (or an increase in existing acne). This can be affected by hygiene. However, teens with good hygiene can still develop acne, and washing their face won't necessarily make it better. If your teen develops acne, it's a good idea to speak to a dermatologist. Although acne usually diminishes with time, it's not guaranteed to go away, and could cause scarring if not treated.

Some parents worry about "roid rage"; that is, the idea that a teen taking prescribed testosterone might get more angry than usual, or even violent. This belief arose because of anecdotal and research evidence that some bodybuilders taking illegal anabolic steroids experience increased anger.

However, people who abuse steroids for fitness reasons usually have testosterone levels several times higher than the typical cis male range. Rest assured that your transmasculine teen's doctor will not prescribe them a testosterone dosage that puts them out of the typical male range, and will test your teen's testosterone levels regularly. Your teen is no more likely to have roid rage on testosterone than your average cis teenage male. Some trans teens experience emotional changes, such as less tearfulness, but rage is an unlikely one.

All about Estrogen (and Androgen Blockers)

Estrogen is usually prescribed as a pill (which can either be administered sublingually—under the tongue—or swallowed), but it can also be administered in injectable, implant, or patch form. Transfeminine teens are typically also prescribed androgen blockers, such as spironolactone, finasteride, and/or cyproterone, in order to block the production of testosterone and the body changes it produces. These are usually taken in pill form.

The most common effects of estrogen are breast growth, redistribution of fat in the face and body, slower growth of facial and body hair, decreased muscle mass, and softening and thinning of skin. Sometimes, hormone therapy for transfeminine teens can have emotional effects. For example, some transfeminine people report greater emotional range than before hormone therapy.

Estrogen and androgen blockers are unlikely to change your teen's voice significantly and won't completely stop facial or body hair growth if it has already started. Many transfeminine teens choose to have surgical or aesthetic procedures to address these issues. You can read about these procedures on page 95 ("Understanding Gender Affirming Surgeries and Other Procedures").

All about Puberty Blockers

Puberty blockers are medications that prevent the body from producing sex hormones. Before puberty blockers began to be used to delay puberty in transgender youth, they were commonly prescribed for children who began puberty prematurely. They are usually injectable but can take the form of an implant. These drugs are often known by brand names such as Lupron.

These medications can prevent the often-irreversible changes that usually happen during puberty, like breast growth, menstruation, hip widening, voice deepening, facial structure changes, and facial/body hair growth. Blockers can give teens and pre-teens more time to figure out whether they'd like to go through endogenous puberty (the type of puberty typical to their assigned gender) or begin gender-affirming hormone therapy for a different kind of puberty.

However, the effects of puberty blockers are completely reversible. Your child can decide to stop using them at any time and go through endogenous puberty. Studies done to date on the physical and psychological effects of puberty blockers suggest overwhelmingly positive effects and few drawbacks.

Questions You Might Be Afraid to Ask: Can Transgender Teens on Hormone Therapy Still Get Pregnant or Get Someone Pregnant?

Yes to both questions.

For people who can get pregnant, testosterone is not a contraceptive. Your teen will not lose their ability to get pregnant if they start gender-affirming hormone therapy, assuming their uterus and ovaries are functioning typically. Testosterone will reduce their fertility but will not eliminate it completely. Teens who have a penis and testes can still cause someone to become pregnant, even after starting hormone therapy—which will reduce their fertility but not eliminate it.

If a teen with ovaries and a uterus has penis-in-vagina (PIV) sex with someone with a penis and testes, pregnancy can result.

However, pregnancy from anal sex, oral sex, or touching with hands is not possible. Teens without a uterus or ovaries cannot get pregnant at all, and teens without a penis and testes cannot cause someone else to become pregnant, regardless of any surgical procedures they might have undergone. (Forgive me if all that sounds obvious, but it's a warning born of experience.)

Talk to your teen about contraceptive methods that can prevent them or their partner from becoming pregnant, such as internal or external condoms, hormonal contraception (e.g., contraceptive pills, patches, or implants), diaphragms, and IUDs. Your teen's health-care provider will be able to recommend contraception that works for your teen's age, assigned gender at birth, and health history.

Turn to the Resources section (page 126) to learn about how to find trans-affirming health care for your teen, including sexual health clinics that can educate you and your teen about contraception, prescribe or recommend contraceptives, and provide trans-competent OB/GYN care.

Parenting Tips and Conversation Starters: How to Use Empathy to Talk to Your Teen about Hormone Therapy

You've been out of your teenage years for a while now, and it might be hard to remember how you once felt about your body. Perhaps it doesn't seem like this has anything to do with your teen's decision about whether to undergo gender-affirming hormone therapy. But accessing these emotions—the needs and longings of teenagerhood—might help you understand what your teen is going through. Even if you can't fully understand what might be happening inside your teen's head, you've probably had experiences that are more or less similar.

Here are some exercises to tap into your past that might help you talk to your teen about hormone therapy in an empathetic way:

- Think about a time when you were impatient to grow up and look like an adult. Did you want a bigger chest? A deeper, manlier voice? Abs like Brad Pitt? A nice butt? Your teen probably wants a few of these things, too.

- Think about a time when you wanted something the adults around you didn't understand. Maybe your parents didn't get why you wanted to be a lawyer when taking over the family roofing business seemed like a much safer path. Perhaps you wanted to play Dungeons and Dragons while your mom insisted you join the cheer squad. Your teen might have the same feelings about the things you want for them.

- Think about a time when you were struggling to make a decision. The adults around you probably had a lot of advice. Some of their advice might have been useful, but you might have also felt that they were thinking about their own needs and goals, not yours. Your teen might have some of the same thoughts about their own decisions.

- Think about the relationship you have with your parents now. Are there things you can't talk to your parents about? Aspects of your life you keep from them? Topics you know not to bring up? Thinking back to your teenage years, what might they have done to make you feel more comfortable talking about these things? Your teen wants to be able to connect with you, just as you might have wanted to be understood by your parents, even when you disagreed.

Understanding Gender-Affirming Surgeries and Other Procedures

Gender-affirming surgery is an umbrella term for any surgical procedure that enhances someone's happiness and comfort with their body in relation to their gender identity. You might also hear terms like *gender reassignment surgery* or *gender confirmation surgery*. (But do not use outdated and inaccurate terms like *sex change*!)

You might have also heard terms like *top surgery* and *bottom surgery*. These are also umbrella terms that refer to a variety of procedures. Top surgery refers to surgery on the chest, and bottom surgery refers to genital surgery. There are other types of surgery that don't fall into these categories, and we'll talk about them in a moment. There are also non-surgical aesthetic procedures, such as hair removal, that might make your teen feel more confident in their body. Although these surgeries are categorized in this book as "transfeminine" and "transmasculine," keep in mind that not everyone who seeks gender-affirming surgery uses these labels.

As with hormone therapy, your teen will usually need a letter of support from a gender therapist to have gender-affirming surgery. The assessment process for surgery will likely be longer and more thorough than for hormone therapy. The requirements for this letter will be different depending on the type of surgery, age of your teen, and the individual requirements of the therapist and the surgeon. Some surgeons only work with teens over the age of 18, and others will perform certain procedures on teens ages 16 or 17.

Most surgical procedures will involve several days, if not weeks, of post-surgical care after your teen is discharged from the hospital. After this initial period, your teen will need to take a break from some tasks, such as running errands and doing household chores. Your family can provide post-surgical care if you and your teen are comfortable with it. Or you can arrange to hire a trained professional to help, which may be covered by your teen's health insurance. Your teen's surgeon may be able to recommend a home health-care agency that can provide trans-knowledgeable care.

How do trans teens and their parents choose which surgeon to work with? For most teens, results are important. Some surgeons provide photos of their surgical results on their websites, and others provide them upon request. And trans people often share photos and videos of their surgical results on forums and social media sites (hat tip to the Resources section on page 126 for info on some of these sites, and for information about finding a surgeon). You and your teen may also consider factors like bedside manner, cost, types of procedures performed, health insurance acceptance, and the need to travel.

In the next section, we'll talk about some of the most common procedures your teen might decide to undergo now or in the future. And if you and your teen are interested in exploring these options with surgeons and other providers, you can find directories of these providers on page 126.

Surgery Options for Transfeminine People

Vaginoplasty is a procedure that involves the surgical creation of a vagina. There are many different vaginoplasty techniques for both binary and nonbinary transfeminine people, and your teen and their surgeon can collaboratively decide which one is best for them. The recovery time for this procedure can involve up to a week in the hospital and as long as six weeks at home. During that time, your teen will be restricted in the activities they can perform, and will need help from a family member, friend, or nurse with such tasks as changing dressings, keeping the incisions clean, and using the bathroom.

Breast augmentation is performed when gender-affirming hormone therapy does not result in breasts that are as proportional with your teen's body as your teen would like (or if your teen decides not to undergo hormone therapy at all). Usually, surgeons require that patients, if receiving hormone therapy, allow enough time for estrogen to affect breast growth before receiving breast augmentation, so this surgery is not common in trans teens under 18. The recovery period for breast augmentation is shorter and less intense than for vaginoplasty, but your teen will still require help from another person, especially with physical tasks that involve lifting their arms.

Facial feminization involves creating a more feminine facial appearance by changing certain features, like the brow, chin, jaw, nose, trachea (Adam's apple), and cheekbones. Rest assured, your teen will still look like themself. The changes of facial feminization surgery are subtle but can greatly boost your teen's confidence in their appearance.

Laryngoplasty (sometimes called *voice surgery*) involves surgery on the voice box to raise your teen's speaking pitch, which can help them feel more comfortable speaking and make it less likely that they'll be misgendered in person or on the telephone. Your teen will need to plan not to use their voice for up to a month after surgery. Another option your teen might use to change the sound of their voice is *voice training*, which can be done with a voice coach or speech therapist, and is often done prior to, after, or instead of laryngoplasty. Some transfeminine people train their voices on their own using apps or videos to practice, but it's usually easier with the help of a professional.

Some transfeminine teens decide to undergo *body sculpting* (also called *body contouring*) if they feel that gender-affirming hormone therapy hasn't provided them with enough of a feminine shape (or if they don't want hormone therapy). These procedures can alter the size and shape of your teen's midsection, hips, and buttocks. If your teen is currently on hormone therapy, these procedures are usually delayed until estrogen has had enough time to feminize their body fat distribution.

Permanent hair removal is a non-surgical procedure that can be performed on the face and body by trained professionals, such as electrologists and laser technicians. The most popular types of hair removal are *electrolysis* and *laser hair removal*. Electrolysis involves using electricity to destroy hair follicles, and laser hair removal does the same with light. Both procedures usually require multiple visits. Hair removal can be temporarily painful, but numbing creams and over-the-counter pain medications can often be used.

Some teens opt for *temporary hair removal,* such as waxing, tweezing, or hair removal creams, which can be performed either by an aesthetician at a spa or salon, or by your teen at home. Home hair removal can be safe and effective, but your teen should always read the directions and test one small patch of skin before moving to the rest of the body, as these products can cause irritation or allergic reactions.

Surgery Options for Transmasculine People

Mastectomy (also called *top surgery* or *chest surgery*) involves removing the breasts and constructing a masculine-appearing chest. There are many techniques that offer different aesthetic results and are appropriate for different body types. The recovery process takes between one and two weeks. During that time (and possibly to some degree afterward), your teen will have physical restrictions and will not be able to lift their arms above their head or perform strenuous physical tasks. Some trans people use *tattooing* to change the appearance of their nipples and areolae, to create the appearance of nipples if they choose a surgery option that doesn't include nipple grafts, or to cover up scars.

Phalloplasty (sometimes referred to as *phallo*) and *metoid-ioplasty* (sometimes called *meta* or *meto*) are both procedures that involve the surgical creation of a phallus and sometimes a scrotum and testes. Phalloplasty uses skin and tissue from both the vulva and other sites, such as the arm or thigh, to create a penis. Metoidioplasty involves releasing the ligaments that attach the clitoris to the body, which creates a smaller penis than one created by phalloplasty, typically with more physical sensation. As with vaginoplasty, there are variations to both procedures too numerous to list here. Phalloplasty is performed in several stages, which means multiple trips to the surgical center. Metoidioplasty is usually done in one or two stages. Recovery periods vary based on the stage and type of procedure but are generally in the three- to six-week range. Phalloplasty and metoidioplasty are not usually performed on patients who are under 18.

A transmasculine person may decide to have a *hysterectomy* (removal of the uterus), which can be performed in conjunction with an *oophorectomy* (removal of the ovaries) or *salpingectomy* (removal of the fallopian tubes). These procedures were more commonly performed in the past because of concerns that testosterone could cause increased cancer risk, but more recent research has not found an increased risk. Other reasons for undergoing a hysterectomy may include uterine health problems, contraception, and reducing estrogen production. Although hysterectomies are not usually performed on teens, your teen may be considering undergoing this procedure in the future.

Some transmasculine people undergo *body contouring*. This procedure usually involves liposuction on the hips, buttocks, thighs, or other areas. It can sometimes be done using a local anesthetic or as an outpatient procedure.

Questions You Might Be Afraid to Ask: Why Do Some Trans People Want Hormone Therapy or Gender-Affirmation Surgery While Others Don't?

Many reasons! Every trans person's feelings about their body are different. Trans people who decide not to have surgery or take hormones have different reasons for that decision, and not every trans person who decides to undergo one physical gender-affirming process wants to get every other procedure available to them.

There are often logistical or economic reasons that trans people don't have surgery or take hormones, even if they want to do one or both things in the future. Although health insurance usually covers both hormones and surgery, some trans people aren't insured, or their insurance may not cover the surgeon they want to use. Often, taking time off work or school presents a financial challenge. And hormones often require access to a letter from a therapist, lab work, and physician consults, which can be costly and time-consuming.

Many trans people don't think they would be happy with the results of certain surgeries or are afraid of complications. Surgical techniques are advancing quickly, and trans surgeries are largely safe, but everyone has different views on what kinds of risks are acceptable. And some have health issues that might make surgery or hormones unnecessarily risky.

One of the most common reasons any trans person might decide against surgery is that they're happy with the way their body looks. That might seem strange if you're used to thinking of trans identity solely as unhappiness with one's body. Although that matches the experiences of some trans people, others don't have strong feelings about changing their physical bodies, or they see their appearance (or certain parts of their appearance) as unimportant to their inner experience of gender.

Whether to get surgery and hormones are both big decisions. Your teen might not decide right away. They may have doubts about whether it's right for them, or fears about the effects of surgery or hormones. Seeking out other trans people and listening to their experiences might be a good way for your teen to get comfortable with this decision. It can also be a good idea to speak with a trans-competent primary care doctor, who will have experience with the fears and hopes that come with medical gender affirmation.

Questions You Might Be Afraid to Ask: How Do I Reconcile the Child I Once Knew with This New Person?

It might be hard not to feel as though your teen is a totally new person if they're now going by a different name or pronouns, dressing in different clothes, or have made changes to their physical bodies. And there's absolutely no shame in feeling weird—or even sad—about these changes. But those external factors don't mean their personality has changed, or that they're an entirely different person. Your teen still has the qualities you've always valued—their talents, quirks, habits, and absolute disregard for turning off the lights when they leave a room.

It's true that your teen might be making other changes that go beyond appearance. Your teen may have made new friends in the queer and trans community. They might be trying out new hobbies and activities that may have seemed off limits to them in their assigned gender. It might be startling to see the ways your teen has grown and changed a short time.

$\longrightarrow$

Remember that trans teens aren't the only teens whose personalities and interests change as they get older, sometimes in radical and unexpected ways. As with any teen, growth and change don't mean your teen has become a fundamentally different person. Just as your teen as child was different from the way they were as a toddler, your teen now has experiences behind them that they didn't a year, five years, or a decade ago. They'll be sure to surprise you more in the future in ways that have nothing to do with gender.

Sometimes what parents mean when they say "My teen is a new person" is something more like "I no longer understand or connect with my teen in the way I used to." Or, often, something more akin to "Our relationship has changed in ways that make me sad."

It's tempting to think this has something to do with coming out as trans. However, relationship changes with your trans teen don't mean your teen's identity, or the process of gender affirmation, is at fault. Your teen's gender exploration is also coming at a time when another major change is taking place: a child's process of becoming an adult. It's possible that your image of your teen hasn't kept up with the ways they've changed throughout the years. Maybe they've sensed that you wish they were still the same person they were a year, five years, or ten years ago. Maybe it's tough to connect with your teen when the child you thought you knew isn't the emerging adult you see today.

It's okay to grieve the person your teen used to be. You might cry when you see old photos of your child or think about how you caught them drawing on your wallpaper. Know that this is something that happens to all parents when their children grow up and begin to cultivate their own lives. But also know that your teen is looking for chances to connect with you and to share the new things they've discovered about themself with you.

Parenting Tips and Conversation Starters: How to Deal with Your Anxiety about Discussing Gender-Affirming Surgery

The thought of a trans teen having gender-affirming surgery represents one of the biggest anxieties parents have when their kid comes out as trans. This anxiety might seem rational—after all, we're talking about big, irreversible life changes—but none of this is going to happen right away. You won't look away for a moment and find that your teen has gotten surgery while you were distracted!

In other words, nothing bad is going to happen if you listen to your teen, validate their struggles, and affirm that their concerns are important to you. As you've probably guessed, you can't make your teen more or less trans, or make them want or not want to have surgery, by reacting negatively or anxiously to conversations about gender-affirming surgery. This is true regardless of whether you feel your teen is ready to start considering surgery.

Here are some tips for a smoother conversation around gender-affirming surgery:

- Go with your second reaction. There's no need to blurt out the first thing that comes to your head. Honesty is great, but not when your honest reaction is one that might raise your teen's anxiety levels or put a dent in what is otherwise a close, loving relationship. Take a deep breath and consider whether what you're about to say will help facilitate future dialogue with your teen, even if you feel your concern is 100 percent valid.

- Try not to catastrophize, at least out loud. Understand-ably, your mind might jump to questions like *What if you have unforeseen complications?* or *What if you wake up one day and regret it?* These might be *possible* outcomes, but they're not necessarily the most likely ones. Some of the outcomes that spring to mind might not be very likely at all. And there's almost no chance your teen hasn't thought about these possibilities, so there's no need to add to *their* anxiety. You can have whatever thoughts you'd like in the privacy of your own head, but you don't have to say every one of them.

- Learn to tolerate anxiety. Learn to think of anxiety as a phenomenon that—by itself—*is not danger-ous.* You might feel anxious about the prospect of gender-affirming surgery for your teen, and your worries may be both valid and normal. However, anx-iety *itself* cannot hurt you, and nothing catastrophic will happen if you are anxious about your teen's future without doing anything about it or telling your teen. This means that you don't have to dispel your anxiety by endlessly voicing your worries to your teen, even if that would provide temporary relief. If you feel the need to let your anxieties out, do so with another adult. Excuse yourself to relieve some stress with a low-stakes activity or a trip to the gym. (Or a glass of wine. I won't judge.)

- Seek support. Parents of trans teens often focus on seeking support for their teens even at the expense of their own mental health needs. Your teen certainly needs your support, but the best way to support your teen is to build your capacity to support them. This may involve seeking your own therapy, a support group for parents of trans teens, or just another adult outside your immediate family who can lend an ear.

Key Takeaways

In this chapter, we've discussed some of the most difficult topics for parents of trans teens: sexuality and surgery. You've survived some of my painfully explicit descriptions of bodies, surgeries, and sex—thank goodness *that's* over! But, don't forget:

- Your teen needs comprehensive sex education that includes and affirms trans bodies. There are many educational resources available to them, some of which are listed in the Resources section (page 126).

- Active listening is a tool that can help you have more productive conversations—about sex, gender, and a wide variety of other topics—with your teen.

- Your teen is likely going through many of the things you went through as a teen, even though your experiences were different. Thinking about those times may help you have more empathy for your teen.

- Gender-affirming hormone therapy and surgery can help your trans teen affirm their gender and feel more comfortable in their body. A gender therapist can help them decide what's right for them.

- Not every trans person wants gender-affirming surgery, or wants it right away.

Just by making it as far as you have in this book, you've done a lot to build your ability to support your child. In the next chapter, we'll talk about ways you can continue to create a supportive environment for your teen beyond the physical parts of gender affirmation. We'll look at things you can do in your individual relationship with your teen, in your immediate and extended family, and in your larger community.

CHAPTER 5

It Starts with You: Creating a Supportive and Accepting Environment for Your Teen

Congratulations on getting to the last chapter. You've come a long way, and through topics that are tough for any parent to think and talk about. This chapter is about making your trans teen comfortable in the different spheres they move through as they navigate the changes they're experiencing right now.

We're going to look at some of the ways you can create a supportive environment for your teen—at home, at school, in your family, and in your community. We'll talk about concrete ways you can improve your individual relationship with your teen and let family in on the important aspects of your child's gender identity. We'll also talk about how you can influence your community for the better—for your own child, and the trans teens who might come after them.

You might find that when you get more confident about the way you support your teen individually, you will take on a more active role in advocating for trans issues in the larger world. Many parents of trans teens go on to share their stories with the world, help other parents support their teens, or get involved in activism. Even smaller actions like voting for laws that protect trans people or talking privately with other parents can make a tangible difference. This chapter might give you some ideas on how you can have an impact on the world in which your trans teen will grow up.

What You Can Do One-on-One

Recall that in chapter 1 (page 1), we talked about research that showed that trans teens found it most supportive when their parents simply used the correct name and pronouns. Another thing these researchers found was that teens rated their parents as more supportive than parents rated themselves.

Clearly, there's more to names and pronouns than just calling someone what they want to be called. What these teens likely saw in their parents wasn't just the willingness to respond to their needs, but also the recognition of who they were. Those parents were saying, in essence, *I see you.*

There will be plenty of opportunities to "see" your teen in the coming months and years. Recognizing the importance of the changes they've made, and looking upon these changes as positive and joyful, is one of them. Expressing appreciation for your teen's honesty and bravery in coming to you for support is another. And another is asking your teen questions about their experiences and genuinely wanting to know the answers—not just to support them, but also to know more about your teen for the sheer joy of knowing.

Helping your teen find outside support is just as important. Part of "seeing" your teen clearly is also seeing your own limitations, and the limitations of being a parent in general. Neither you nor your teen will be able to navigate this process on your own. However your teen decides they need to embrace and express their gender, they'll need some combination of family support, peer support, school support, therapy, and other gender-affirming health care. And you'll need your own support from other parents or professionals.

Embrace Being Wrong

Being honest and vulnerable with your teen about your uncertainties and opening yourself up to the possibility of mistakes are two of the most powerful things you can do as a parent. Being open to being wrong is not going to feel *right* or resemble some of the common cultural models of American parenthood—for instance, did Mike Brady ever seem like he felt completely adrift as a parent?—but it might be a relief to be able to talk to your teen without feeling as though you have to be absolutely sure about what you're doing.

How can you embrace being wrong as a parent? One way is to be open with your teen about gaps in your knowledge. You might feel the need to be firm and consistent, perhaps feeling that you'll confuse your teen by appearing uncertain, but a consistent parent can also be a curious, interested parent. Let your teen know when you don't know something. Tell your teen when you're not exactly sure what to do, and make sure they understand that you're open to new information. This will not only help your teen feel as though you're accepting of new ideas they might bring to you, but also model what an inquisitive, open-minded adult looks like.

Another way to get comfortable with being wrong is to examine your own motives. Did you fret about your teen wearing a skirt to the Halloween party because you thought they'd get bullied, or was it because your judgmental sister would be there? Is your teen's gender exploration happening too quickly, or is it just too quickly for *you*? There's no need to beat yourself up if you realize you might need to re-center your teen's perspective. Looking at the reasons for your own behavior and self-correcting makes you a self-aware parent.

One final way you can embrace being wrong is by questioning the things you believe—and not just about gender. Your teen's discoveries about their gender might have opened up uneasy questions about parenting, relationships, family, and life itself. Instead of trying to reassure yourself that the things your parents ingrained in you as a child were completely without error—which, while it might be comforting, gives you no new knowledge or insight—try following the path those questions may lead you to. Turn to the tips on page 112 ("How to Show Up Imperfectly for Your Teen") to learn how to embrace being wrong and making mistakes.

Questions You Might Be Afraid to Ask: What Does It Mean If Another One of My Children Comes Out as Trans? Can Trans People Have Trans Siblings?

Sure. Statistically, given that a little under half a percent of the population is trans, it's no surprise that some trans people also have trans siblings—in the same way that many gay people, left-handed people, and people who love model trains also have siblings who are gay, left-handed, or have similar hobbies. Famous trans siblings include Lana and Lilly Wachowski, directors of *The Matrix* and other blockbuster films.

If you have a trans child who is the younger sibling of another trans child, you might wonder whether one sibling came out as trans because the other one did. But it's impossible to influence someone to identify as trans by example. I've worked with several trans people who were siblings of other trans people, and I can assure you that none of them suddenly "decided" to be trans because their siblings were trans.

In fact, many trans people are *more* reluctant to come out after their sibling comes out, often fearing that their parents will think they're copying their sibling. And some trans people with trans siblings see how their family reacts to their sibling coming out and delay coming out themselves because the family's reaction is negative or invalidating.

This is why it's especially important to create a supportive environment, reflect on your own behavior and beliefs, demonstrate self-awareness and self-correct, and be careful about the language you use about gender and the way you talk about trans people. Even if your transgender teen's siblings all turn out to be cisgender, they'll take their cues about how to treat trans people from you.

Parenting Tips and Conversation Starters: How to Show Up Imperfectly for Your Teen

The one rule about parenting a trans teen is that you will inevitably make a mistake. You are not infallible, and sadly, there's no fairy godmother who shows up when your teen comes out as trans and hands you a magic textbook on how to be an amazing parent. (At best, you get a therapist in Queens writing a parenting book in his pajamas.)

The good news is that it's more important to know what to do when you get things wrong than it is to get things right. Why's that? Shouldn't you be focused on getting things right the first time? Ideally, yes, but stressing out about not being perfect might make it harder for you to take risks.

Parenting a trans teen is all about risk. You will start conversations you have no idea how to finish. You will allow your teen to make decisions that fill you with dread. You'll say things that you hope are affirming and supportive but might not be. You'll make assumptions and then you'll correct those assumptions. And you'll risk enduring some of the most tedious, cringeworthy episodes of *RuPaul's Drag Race* in the name of connecting with them.

If you can't take the risk of being an imperfect parent, you might miss opportunities to support your teen because you hesitated, not knowing whether you were saying exactly the right thing. Don't neglect the possibility that being vulnerable and humble about your mistakes could provide opportunities for your teen to learn that you're open to their influence and willing to do better, or that modeling receptiveness to feedback might help your teen become more open and receptive themselves.

Here are some tips on how to show up imperfectly for your teen:

- Get comfortable with the idea that you may have made mistakes in the past in parenting your teen. Assume this has happened more than once. Thinking about these mistakes may make you feel guilty or defensive. But what would you lose by admitting these mistakes? Would your relationship crumble if you told your teen, "I haven't always done the right thing" or "I realize I've been wrong in the past"? Chances are, your teen would welcome the honesty.

- If talking about gender has gotten tense, spend some time together when you're not talking about gender. That doesn't mean you have to shut them down when they talk to you about gender at odd moments, just that you don't have to make every conversation a Big, Important Discussion. You don't need to know everything about gender identity or agree with everything your teen says to take them to a music festival or try out a new restaurant.

- Model vulnerability and imperfection. Talk about mistakes you've made in your life without justifying yourself or shifting the responsibility to someone else. Tell your teen about the ways your beliefs have changed and experiences that have given you new perspectives.

What You Can Do Among Friends and Family

There's no one way to tell family members that your teen is trans, or to help them figure out how to support your teen. The way you help your teen navigate the process of talking to family members about their gender will depend on your teen's own wishes and comfort level.

It will mean having a conversation with your teen first about whom to tell, when to tell them, and how. Perhaps your teen wants to tell Uncle Gerald in person because they're close, but

Cousin Helen gets an email and Grandpa Bob gets a phone call. And maybe some of the more distant relatives and family friends can read about it in a social media post or group text. Your teen might ask you to have these conversations yourself without them present. This may be especially important when your teen isn't sure how a particular relative will react to the news.

There may be people in your family your teen doesn't want to tell or doesn't want to tell right away. Respect your teen's wishes regardless of whether you feel their concerns are justified. You might feel awkward keeping a secret from a relative, especially if you see that person all the time, but your teen's choice about how and when they come out is more important than Aunt Josefa's desire to know the latest about everyone. Your teen is the one who has to deal with the consequences of telling other people, not you or Auntie Jo.

When you talk to relatives about your teen's gender identity, you might want to have an "ask" at the ready. What do you need your relatives to *do*? Do they need to start using a new name or pronoun? Read up on trans identities? Understand what is and is not okay to say to your teen? Write down the answers to these questions so you're prepared. Keeping this "ask" in mind, go into these conversations with concrete solutions, like "Aunt Josefa, my child came out as a boy and goes by Charlie now, and uses he/him pronouns. I'd like you to begin using those pronouns for him, and while I'm happy to answer some questions to clarify things about trans people, please know that any questions about his body are off the table."

Leading by example and presenting specific needs based on your "ask" might relieve any confusion and uncertainty your relatives might have about supporting your teen, and may help them feel as though they can do something specific and concrete rather than wondering what you want them to do.

It might be a good idea to have some brief educational materials on hand to give to relatives so they can learn about the basics: what it means to be transgender, how to support and affirm a trans teen, how to use gender-neutral pronouns, if your teen uses them, and other topics that might be useful to support your teen. The Resources section (page 126) can help you find information about trans identities online, and many of these sites have printable handouts and guides.

When You Need to Have Difficult Conversations

You may be dreading conversations with relatives about your trans teen because you suspect the news won't go over well. Or perhaps you thought your conversations with relatives would be painless, but it turns out Cousin Richie has some ... interesting opinions on trans people. Now you might be wondering what you need to do to make sure your teen isn't harmed or invalidated when they interact with family.

The person in your family making noises about your teen's identity might not be open to changing their opinion. If education doesn't help, you'll need to start setting boundaries. Defining your boundaries internally before you have to enforce them will help you clarify what you can and cannot accept about your family member's behavior: "I don't need Richie to fully accept and understand the existence of trans people, but I do need him to call my child 'she' at Thanksgiving."

There are no boundaries without consequences, so figure out what happens if those boundaries get crossed. Do you speak up at the Thanksgiving table? Leave early? Spend Christmas somewhere else if Richie's invited? Make a plan, and don't let that plan be "Let my teen deal with Richie's behavior to keep the family peace."

Protecting your teen from a family member whose behavior is harmful to them may mean that this person becomes less present in your life, temporarily or permanently. It might mean letting your teen bow out of family gatherings for a time. If you used to have this relative over to your house all the time, those visits might need to stop for now. As with anything involving your teen's safety and comfort, you'll want to let your teen guide you on this. That doesn't mean you immediately cut Richie out of your family's life forever, but it does mean that you need to limit Richie's impact on your teen. Remember that Richie has the choice to respect your teen, and that choosing not to means he places more importance on behaving the way he likes than on being close to you.

You'll undoubtedly get some pushback from your family when you do any of these things. The Cousin Richies of the world act the way they do because their family and friends enable their behavior. But the test of whether you're able to show up for your teen in the ways that matter isn't whether you support them when things are easy. It's the support you give when you know that you'll be making life complicated for yourself by doing so.

Questions You Might Be Afraid to Ask: What Do I Do if My Spouse/ Parent/Friend Doesn't Accept My Child Is Transgender?

This is a tricky situation because you likely have reasons for maintaining a relationship with this person. You may not feel able to leave the situation as you might if a grocery store clerk was being rude to your teen. A spouse or your teen's other parent may have some level of control over your teen's life, which can make it hard for you to affirm your teen's gender in your home or help your teen get gender-affirming medical care. And even if it's a friend and not a family member, you may not want to throw away the entire friendship, even though it hurts you that they don't understand what you do about your teen.

You might be able to enlist a trusted friend, family member, or medical professional to talk to this person. Sometimes, hearing about gender identity from someone they respect might push them to reconsider, even if the facts you're telling them are the same ones. It might click when they see that someone who seems rational and reasonable is also affirming and respectful of your teen.

Talking about where they get their information might be helpful. Some people don't realize when seemingly innocuous or helpful-sounding information comes from anti-trans groups that seek to use misinformation and cherry-picked data to combat trans people's right to safety, nondiscrimination, and health care. Others aren't good consumers of information and don't have any idea who is responsible for the "facts" they're consuming, or how research performed by scientists who study gender is different from the kind of "research" someone might casually do on the internet. You might be able to get them on board with reputable resources that are sourced from good-quality, peer-reviewed scientific literature.

Finally, you may have to err on the side of protecting your teen. You will have to advocate more strongly for your teen than you ever have. You might need to get outside help and support for your teen without seeking your teen's other parent's permission. And if your spouse or a family member outright mistreats your teen, you may have to start thinking about making changes in the relationship, including a temporary or permanent separation.

Parenting Tips and Conversation Starters: Talking to Your Teen about Their Boundaries

Your teen might be feeling more vulnerable right now than ever. If they're impatient to make needed changes or move forward with gender affirmation, they may feel unable to control anything in their lives. They may be having trouble with bullying or discrimination at school, which might cause them to question their self-worth and wonder whether other people owe them anything at all.

This time in your teen's life is when their ability to set boundaries will be extra important. Here are some tips for helping them do that:

- Help your teen plan for what happens when someone violates a boundary. Fundamentally, a boundary is a line that says, "Here is a line that other people can't cross for the sake of my own comfort and safety." Figure out collaboratively what your teen will do if someone does something that makes them uncomfortable or unsafe, such as sexual harassment. Leave the situation? Tell an adult? Make a plan and revise it if needed.

- Respect the reasonable boundaries your teen sets with you. If your teen's bedroom door is closed, knock and get their permission to enter. If they say they don't want to talk about something and you don't think they're in immediate danger, drop it. If they tell you that something you do bothers them, make an effort to honor their feelings.

- Set boundaries with your teen, too. Although going through the process of gender exploration might mean your teen needs extra understanding and patience from you, it doesn't mean you can't have limits on your teen's behavior. The rules of the house are still in effect.

Do think about why the boundary is there. Are you enforcing this rule for household members' well-being, or because this was a boundary in your own family you never questioned? If the boundary exists for a reason, make sure your teen knows that you expect them to demonstrate empathy and awareness of the people around them by respecting it.

- Model setting your own boundaries with others. If you're constantly dropping everything to put out fires in other people's lives, your teen may unconsciously pick up that they're expected to do that, too. And if you allow people in your life to mistreat you, your teen may learn that mistreatment is just a fact of life, not something they should push back against. Let your teen see you holding the line on the things you're willing to do for others and the behavior you're willing to tolerate.

What You Can Do in Your Community

Your teen's gender exploration probably includes an extensive to-do list. You might have made more phone calls and sent more emails than ever before to your teen's teachers and health-care providers. You may be researching topics online you never thought you'd have to. And you've likely started to learn the legal and social ins and outs of trans life to better support your teen.

If you haven't already, you might start thinking about how you can start to change the way your community interacts with trans youth. If you've made an individual case for a program or service to include your teen, you can also make a case for including trans teens in general.

For example, if your teen's summer camp made an exception to allow him to stay in the boys' cabin instead of the girls', you could ask them to change their policies altogether to allow trans youth to stay in the cabin of their choice. If the nice librarian lets your teen use the staff bathroom at the library, maybe you can advocate to change one of the single-sex bathrooms into a gender-neutral one. Instead of just asking for your teen's name to be changed in their school's computer systems, ask the school to develop a standard policy when a student comes out as trans or to train their staff on gender identity.

While you were looking for resources for yourself and your teen, you may have found parents who had taken the initiative to bring other parents together for support and advocacy. Some parents of trans teens lead groups for other parents, raise funds for local queer and trans organizations, create new organizations and resources where none exist, or take action at the local, state, or federal level for political change.

You can start by figuring out where your talents match the needs of local trans youth. The work you do doesn't have to be public-facing or glamorous to be impactful. Maybe you're so organized that it'd be easy for you to collect spare toiletries from local families for an LGBTQ youth shelter. You might be patient enough to knock on doors to get out the vote against an anti-trans bathroom bill. Or you may be a persuasive enough writer to apply for a grant for a local queer arts group.

Every Action Counts

When you think about what you can do for trans youth in your community, you might find that you don't have the bandwidth to take big actions for change. That doesn't mean you can't act in smaller ways, or make decisions that uphold values like compassion and justice. Anything from the way you vote and the laws you support to the way you talk about gender with other people can make an impact. In addition to changing your community, you will also affect the way your teen sees you.

Your teen is watching what you do in general, not just the ways you support them in particular. If you accept and encourage your trans teen but vote for politicians who pass laws that hurt people like your teen, you're sending the message that you don't fully believe that trans people deserve the same rights as other people, negating your message of acceptance. And if you take your teen's identity seriously but don't demonstrate respect or empathy for other trans and queer people, your teen may not believe you when you say you support them.

Conversely, if you take the opportunities to show you care about the larger trans community, you will also be showing your teen that you care about them and their rights. Every one of your actions is an opportunity to show your teen the depth of your commitment to their future happiness and safety.

Questions You Might Be Afraid to Ask: What Should I Do if I Think My Child Is Being Discriminated Against in School or at Work?

First, pull back a bit. What is your teen asking you to do? Respect your teen's right to decide whether and how you intervene. They know their school or workplace better than you do and will have to live with the consequences if your intervention inadvertently worsens their conditions.

Second, make sure you and your teen know their rights. Depending on where you live, your teen may have protections on the federal, state, and/or municipal level to express their gender without discrimination or harassment in the workplace, in public accommodations, or at school. You may not have to invoke these laws or the enforcement mechanisms behind them, but it's useful to know what they are. You can find out where to learn about trans rights, how you and your teen can take action if their rights are violated, how to find legal help,

$\longrightarrow$

and what government agencies can offer help in the Resources section (page 126).

Finally, be prepared for advocacy to be an ongoing process. You may not be able to get your teen's needs met with a single visit or phone call. You might have to talk to several different departments in your teen's school, or go higher up in the chain at your teen's volunteer organization if the people you contact initially can't help you. Continuing to fight for your teen and not losing momentum when things get complicated is a powerful way to communicate that you care.

Parenting Tips and Conversation Starters: Talking to Your Teen about When You Should Intervene

When your teen comes to you with an interpersonal problem related to their gender identity, you might have one of two very common reactions. The first is to step in and address the problem yourself. The second is to step back and let your teen handle it themselves.

Neither reaction is necessarily the right one in all circumstances. There will be times when an adult needs to intervene, and times when you'll need to encourage more autonomy and independence. Here are some tips on how to decide whether to step in to help your teen:

- Is their physical safety in danger? If so, you'll probably want to err on the side of intervening. If not, though, think about stepping back and letting them make their own decisions about how to handle it, even if you're worried.

- Has your teen tried to solve the problem themselves? If not, don't assume that your intervention is necessary.

- Has your teen asked you to intervene to solve the problem? Don't think that because they're telling you the problem, they necessarily need you to fix it. Go by what they ask you to do, not what you think needs to be done.

- Do you actually know how to solve the problem? Get all the information you can from your teen before attempting to intervene.

- Does it seem like a larger issue than just one incident? For example, does one instance of bullying at your child's school point to a larger problem of bullies getting away with mistreating other students? If so, you might want to have a talk with someone in authority who can make larger changes, not just address the most recent instance.

- Given their age and individual strengths, what are your teen's capabilities when it comes to problem-solving? A 13-year-old's capacity to help themselves is different from that of a 17-year-old. Make sure you respect your teen's ability to solve problems and to assert themself.

Key Takeaways

As you work to support your teen in different settings, remember:

- Supporting your teen means recognizing your own limitations and knowing when to get outside help.

- Fear of doing the wrong thing might hinder your ability to support your teen. Embrace being wrong. Learn from it and accept your teen's feedback.

- When you demonstrate self-awareness and correct yourself when you err, you are creating (however imperfectly!) a supportive environment for your trans teen *and* your other children. Your kids and other family members will take cues from you about how to treat trans people.

- Let your teen guide you on whether they need your help in tackling a problem, or if you need to stand back and let them handle it.

- Allow your teen to take the lead on how and when to come out to family members and friends.

- You may have to have difficult conversations with unsupportive or invalidating relatives. The measure of your support of your teen isn't in how you act when things are easy, but how you support your teen when you need to do things that are uncomfortable for you.

- Anything you can do for trans rights, however small, has the potential to make life better for your local trans community.

This might be the end of the main section of this book, but it isn't the end of the book. Remember that Resources section I'm always telling you about? It's coming up on page 126, and will point you to organizations that support trans teens, places to buy gender-affirming clothing, directories that can help you and your teen find trans-friendly health care, and all kinds of other helpful information.

The Journey Forward

Thank you for letting me help guide you through this tough, joyful, frustrating, happy, strange, and exciting time in your life. I'm grateful for the opportunity to answer your questions, provide you with tips to help your life as a parent go more smoothly, and point you toward the information you need to support your teen.

Picking up this book and working your way through its chapters was no easy task. Just by doing that, you've shown a willingness to open your mind to new possibilities and let your teen be your guide. Your life as a parent of a trans individual has just started, and your engagement with this book has provided you with a foundation from which to continue learning and growing.

You don't have to put this book down right away. You can use it as a reference when you're not sure how to answer a question or talk with your teen about thorny gender topics. And you can always flip to the Resources section (page 126) if you're at a loss for where to find information and support, either for yourself or your teen.

I wish you and your teen the best of luck and the closest of relationships in this time.

Resources

Trans Health and Mental Health Care

Finding a trans-competent therapist or other health-care provider for your teen can be a challenge, but many national and local resources can make it easier for you and your family.

- You can often find providers through a referral from your local LGBTQ center or youth center (which can also be a great place for your teen to find support and community). You can find many of these centers through CenterLink at LGBTCenters.org/LGBTCenters.

- The largest online professional directories for mental health professionals are PsychologyToday.com, GoodTherapy.org, and TherapyDen.com. These sites allow you to filter by insurance, specialty, language, age of client, and other considerations.

- The World Professional Association for Transgender Health (WPATH) provider directory at WPATH.org /provider/search lists over a hundred therapists around the world as well as primary care doctors, surgeons, and other providers who are members of that organization. Note that although WPATH offers a certification program in transgender health and allows site users to filter by certified providers, many competent providers do not hold this certification.

- Sites maintained by volunteer members of the trans community include TransCareSite.org (all providers), HealthyTrans.com (surgical and insurance information), MyTransHealth.com (all providers), and TransHealthcare .org (surgeons only).

- GLMA.org maintains a directory with health-care providers who have identified themselves as LGBTQ-friendly.

Your teen may benefit from having these crisis hotlines on hand:

- The Trans Lifeline, at 1-877-565-8860, is staffed with trans peer counselors only. They are open 24/7 and guaranteed to have staff available from 10 a.m. to 4 a.m. EST. The Trans Lifeline has a policy against calling the police or emergency services without the caller's consent.

- Volunteer counselors at the Trevor Project, an LGBTQ crisis line, are available 24/7. Just call 1-866-488-7386 or text START to 678-678. Your teen can also visit TheTrevorProject.org for chat support.

- The LGBT National Help Center can be reached at 1-888-843-4564.

- The National Domestic Violence Hotline is available 24 hours a day at 1-800-799-7233. Callers can also chat with a counselor at TheHotline.org or text LOVEIS to 1-866-331-9474.

- RAINN (Rape, Abuse & Incest National Network) is an organization supporting survivors of sexual violence. They offer 24/7 help via their hotline at 1-800-654-HOPE (4673), and via chat at RAINN.org. They also offer additional resources to adults who suspect a child may be in danger or being harmed.

Support for Parents and Families

Organizations and websites that provide support for families of trans teens include:

- PFLAG is an organization with more than 400 local chapters that provides support to families with LGBTQ children and teens, including support groups. You can find your local chapter at PFLAG.org/find-a-chapter.

- GLSEN advocates for LGBTQ students, with a network of 43 chapters, and offers incredible resources for students and educators (including lesson plans) to help create a safe and supportive classroom environment. Read more at GLSEN.org.

- GenderSpectrum.org provides a wide variety of resources and information, including online groups, for family members looking to learn more about gender identity and provide a supportive environment for their kids.

- New York's LGBT Center maintains online and in-person support groups for trans people and their families. They also offer a vast number of resources. Visit them at GayCenter.org.

- MyKidIsGay.com has resources and support for parents of LGBTQ children and teens and includes many resources for parents of trans kids.

- Trans Student Educational Resources, run by and for transgender youth, offers many resources, infographics, scholarships, and more. Contact them at TransStudent.org.

If you're looking for concise, easily readable information to give to family members, you can visit:

- Trans Youth Equality Foundation (TransYouthEquality .org/for-parents)

- Movement Advancement Project (LGBTMap.org /advancing-acceptance-for-parents)

- Family Acceptance Project (FamilyProject.sfsu.edu)

Sexuality and Sexual Health

Trans-inclusive information for teens (and for adults, too!) about sexuality can be found at:

- Scarleteen (Scarleteen.com)

- Go Ask Alice (GoAskAlice.columbia.edu)

- Planned Parenthood (PlannedParenthood.org)

Planned Parenthood provides many free or affordable services related to trans health care and sexual and reproductive health at locations around the United States and via telehealth. You can call 1-800-230-PLAN or visit PlannedParenthood.org /health-center to find your local health center.

Gender-Affirming Surgery

Some of the best ways to find results photos of gender-affirming surgeries include:

- Transbucket.com allows users to upload photos of their surgery results. Users can filter by type of surgery, surgeon, and many other criteria.

- TopSurgery.net provides general information about transmasculine chest surgery and links to photos of surgery results.

- The subreddit at reddit.com/r/Transgender_Surgeries allows users to upload their results photos.

- Most gender-affirming surgeons will provide photos of their results, either online for public viewing or if you email them.

Be aware that most of these sites are graphic and contain images of nude bodies and surgical procedures. Also, be aware that many results photos display images of surgical results that are not fully healed and do not accurately demonstrate what the results will look like weeks or months later.

Identification Documents
Different states have different requirements for name changes, and some documents—like your teen's passport or Social Security card—must be changed with federal agencies. The National Center for Transgender Equality provides a helpful tool to figure out your state's laws and the procedures for gender marker changes. Visit TransEquality.org/documents for more information.

As these processes can be costly, the Transgender Legal Defense and Education Fund helps low-income people through The Name Change Project, providing pro bono legal services from top law firms. Find out more at TransgenderLegal.org /our-work/name-change-project.

Camps for Trans Youth
Several summer camps across the U.S. provide affirming, supportive environments for trans youth, where they can meet other young trans people and learn outdoor skills in a laid-back, fun setting. Some offer scholarships for families who cannot afford camp.

- Camp Aranu'tiq (New Hampshire, CampAranutiq.org)

- Camp Lilac (Ohio, CampLilac.org)

- Camp Ten Trees (Washington, CampTenTrees.org /summer-camp)

- TYEF Camp (New England, TransYouthEquality.org /youth-retreats-camps)

Other camps for LGBTQ youth can be found at PFLAG.org /youthcamps.

Swimwear, Sportswear, Clothing, and Undergarments

Outplay (OutplayBrand.com), Chromat (Chromat.co), Hirsuit (hirsuit.co) and Rebirth Garments (RebirthGarments.com) sell swimwear and sportswear for all genders.

High-quality binders can be purchased from GC2B (GC2B.co), FLAVNT Streetwear (FLAVNT.com), and Shapeshifters (ShapeShifters.co). Point of Pride (PointOfPride.org/chest-binder -donations) provides free binders and other gear to people who cannot afford or safely obtain them. In Canada, Gender Gear (GenderGear.ca/products/preloved-binders) offers a binder recycling program that provides pre-owned binders for $10, and Vancouver's Qmunity offers a binder exchange program for youth at Qmunity.ca/get-support/youth/bbbexchange.

TransGuySupply.com offers a variety of transmasculine-geared products, such as packers and packing underwear.

Trans Tool Shed (transtoolshed.com) offers many products for both transfeminine and transmasculine people, including breast prosthetics, pocket bras, tucking underwear and supplies, shapewear, binders, packers/harnesses, stand-to-pee devices, clothing, and books.

Undergarments and prosthetics for transfeminine people, including tucking underwear, can also be found at Origami Customs (OrigamiCustoms.com), and En Femme (EnFemmeStyle.com). However, En Femme is not a trans-owned business; the site also sells products targeted toward cross-dressers, drag queens, and other people whose identities do not necessarily intersect with the trans community. To that end, there are also sellers on Amazon who provide products like these, in a similar context.

Point of Pride (PointOfPride.org/trans-femme-shapewear) collaborates with Origami Customs to offer free shapewear for transfeminine people who cannot afford or safely obtain it. Vancouver's Qmunity also has a bra and breast form exchange program for youth at Qmunity.ca/get-support/youth /bbbexchange.

Info on tucking safely can be found at PrideInPractice.org /articles/transgender-genital-tucking-guide, Buzzfeed.com /meredithtalusan/all-the-questions-you-had-about-tucking -but-were-afraid-to-a, and PointOfPride.org/trans-femme -shapewear/#tucking-resources.

A guide to finding tall and plus-size women's clothing and shoes at major retailers can be found at TransgenderMap.com /social/tall-clothing (though note the website is outdated in its language, and isn't always inclusive of non-femme transfeminine identities). Buzzfeed's tall women's clothing recommendation is also useful: Buzzfeed.com/allisonjiang/best-places-to-buy-clothes-for-tall-people. Stores and brands with extended sizing include Asos, Old Navy, Nordstrom, Universal Standard, Torrid, and Long Tall Sally.

National clothing, underwear, and makeup stores with trans-friendly policies and trans-inclusive or gender-neutral fitting rooms include Nordstrom, Target, Macy's, American Eagle /Aerie, Gap Inc. brands (which include Old Navy, Banana Republic, and Athleta), Abercrombie & Fitch, Sephora, Lush, and MAC.

Many products created by and for trans people can be found by searching sites that sell handmade products, such as Etsy.com.

Clothing Alterations

Although there are a handful of trans-friendly tailors at various price points in most major cities, it may be a little more difficult to find someone in your area. If you've got an old Singer gathering dust, well, now's the time to take it out of the basement and work with your teen on modifying and crafting clothes at home.

The Trans Sewing Project (TransSewingProject.WordPress .com) is a site created by a member of the trans community about sewing and patternmaking for trans bodies. This site can help you or your teen alter garments and even create new ones. Sites like Sewing.com and SewGuide.com have easy how-to guides on how to do many common alterations.

The Canadian health clinic Trans Care BC maintains a resource for DIY-ing some common gender-affirming undergarments and safely binding, packing, tucking, and padding using common pieces of clothing or household objects: PHSA.ca /transcarebc/care-support/transitioning/bind-pack-tuck-pad.

Discrimination at School or Work

If your teen faces discrimination at school, they can file a complaint with the US Department of Education at this site: ED.gov /about/offices/list/ocr/complaintintro.html. The National Center for Transgender Equality has information about your teen's rights at school and actions to take if they face discrimination at transequality.org/know-your-rights/schools.

If your teen experiences workplace discrimination, they can file a charge with the US Equal Employment Opportunity Commission (EEOC) at EEOC.gov/filing-charge-discrimination. They may also file with their state or local government (which may offer more protections) instead. The state agencies charged with enforcing these laws are called Fair Employment Practices Agencies (FEPAs); you can usually find your local FEPA by Googling "[your state or city] employment discrimination." The National Center for Transgender Equality (TransEquality.org) has information about your teen's rights at work as well.

The Transgender Law Center (TransgenderLawCenter. org) and the Sylvia Rivera Law Project (SRLP.org) can provide assistance, referral, and resources to people experiencing gender identity-related legal issues.

Religious Resources

If you're struggling to accept your teen's gender identity for religious reasons, or if your teen is having a religious crisis as a result of the feelings they're having about their gender, there are many resources online that might help you reconcile your family's beliefs and your teen's identity.

Gay Church maintains a directory of LGBTQ-affirming Christian churches searchable by address at GayChurch.org /find_a_church. QueerTheology.com is a website with resources to help LGBTQ Christians and their families embrace their sexuality and gender identity. Their resources on trans identity and Christian theology can be found at QueerTheology.com /transgender. Middle Church in New York's East Village is a leading inclusive and progressive ministry; they broadcast their services online every Sunday. Their LGBTQ resource list is available at MiddleChurch.org/lgbtqia-justice-resources.

The Muslim Alliance for Sexual and Gender Diversity (MuslimAlliance.org) is an organization that advocates for LGBTQ Muslims. Advocates for Youth (AdvocatesForYouth. org) has produced a guide for young Muslims who are questioning their gender called "I'm a Muslim and My Gender Doesn't Fit Me: Resources for Trans Muslim Youth." It's available at AdvocatesForYouth.org/wp-content/uploads/2019/05 /Im-Muslim-My-Gender-Doesnt-Fit-Me.pdf.

Eshel (EshelOnline.org) is an organization in New York City that provides support to Orthodox Jewish LGBTQ people and their families. They maintain a warmline at 1-724-374-3501. Jewish Queer Youth (JQYouth.org) is another resource for Jewish trans teens and their families, with a focus on Sephardic and Orthodox communities. Keshet (KeshetOnline.org) is an organization that promotes LGBTQ equality in the Jewish community and offers resources and events. TransTorah.org is a site about

Jewish texts and traditions that may help you find clarity about how your teen's identity might fit with your Jewish faith. Congregation Beit Simchat Torah, based on New York, is the world's largest LGBTQ synagogue, and maintains a resource page for transgender Jews at CBST.org/transjews. Other resources can be found at PFLAG.org/jewish.

Gender Identity in Media

Here's a short list of documentaries, podcasts, and TV specials in order of year released. Although there are many films and TV shows about trans people, this list was chosen specifically to highlight positive, accurate, and uplifting portrayals of trans lives, issues relevant to young trans people and their families, and the wide range of identities and experiences in the trans community.

All these works are appropriate for teens, which means you and your teen might want to watch them together. Some deal with sexuality, medical treatment, discrimination, hate crimes, death, and other sensitive topics. If you or your teen are sensitive to these subjects, you might want to type the title of the film into a site like DoesTheDogDie.com to see what type of material it contains.

You can find other films and videos, many from small and independent creators, at TransgenderMediaPortal.org. And if you and your teen are interested in attending a trans film festival or watching films from these festivals, you can find them at TransgenderMediaPortal.org/trans_film_festivals.

- *Paris Is Burning* (1990) follows the lives of black and Latinx trans and queer members of New York City's ballroom culture in the 1980s, and was one of the inspirations for FX's *Pose*.

- *Southern Comfort* (2001) tells the story of Robert Eads, a trans man dying of ovarian cancer who is determined to make one last appearance at a large transgender gathering in the deep South.

- *Just Call Me Kade* (2002) is a documentary about a trans teenager whose family embraces his identity.

- *Screaming Queens* (2005) is a documentary about the 1966 Compton's Cafeteria riots, a watershed moment for trans rights in the U.S. It was written and directed by Susan Stryker, a preeminent trans historian.

- *True Trans with Laura Jane Grace* (2014) is a documentary web series covering punk singer/songwriter Laura Jane Grace, of the band Against Me!, during her first two years of being out as trans.

- *I Am Jazz* (2015–) is a TV series that follows the life of Jazz Jennings, a transgender teenage girl.

- *Becoming More Visible* (2016) showcases the experiences of four trans youth.

- *We Exist: Beyond the Binary* (2018) is a documentary about nonbinary life that tells the story of Lauren, a nonbinary adult in their twenties, and features other nonbinary people, as well as doctors who work with gender-variant people.

- *Science VS*: "The Science of Being Transgender" (2018) is a podcast episode in Gimlet Media's *Science VS* series about research on trans identities featuring two psychologists and an endocrinologist. You can listen to it for free at GimletMedia.com/shows/science-vs/j4hl23.

- *Born to Be* (2019) is a documentary about the work of surgeon Dr. Jess Ting and other clinicians at the Mount Sinai Center for Transgender Medicine and Surgery.

- *Disclosure: Trans Lives On Screen* (2020) is a documentary film made by and starring trans people, which discusses and critiques how mainstream Hollywood presents trans lives.

- *No Ordinary Man* (2020) is the story of Billy Tipton, a transmasculine musician in the 1940s and 1950s, whose identity was revealed at his death in the typical shock journalism of the late 1980s. Written by and starring many well-known advocates and actors, Tipton's story is reclaimed by trans community in a historical exploration of trans identity that also models healthy trans lives and transmasculine kinship.

Here is a list of books by trans authors featuring trans subjects and themes. All the books on this list are enjoyable for both teens and adults. Sensitive readers should note that some of these books describe sexuality, violence, and other mature content.

Fiction

- *Cemetery Boys*, Aiden Thomas

- *Felix Ever After*, Kacen Callender

- *I Wish You All The Best*, Mason Deaver

- *Little Fish*, Casey Plett

- *Nevada*, Imogen Binnie

- *Pet*, Akwaeke Emezi

Nonfiction

- *A Quick & Easy Guide to Queer & Trans Identities*, Mady G. and Jules Zuckerberg

- *Gender Outlaw*, Kate Bornstein

- *Gender Queer: A Memoir* (graphic novel), Maia Kobabe

- *Trans Bodies, Trans Selves*, Laura Erickson-Schroth (Ed.)

- *Transgender History*, Susan Stryker

References

Arnoldussen, Marijn, Thomas Steensma, Arne Popma, Anna van der Miesen, Jos W. R. Twisk, and Annelou de Vries. "Re-evaluation of the Dutch Approach: Are Recently Referred Transgender Youth Different Compared to Earlier Referrals?" *European Child & Adolescent Psychiatry* 29, no. 6 (August 2019): 803–811. DOI.org/10.1007/s00787 -019-01394-6.

Becker-Hebly, Inga, Saskia Fahrenkrug, Florentien Campion, Hertha Richter-Appelt, Michael Schulte-Markwort, and Claus Barkmann. "Psychosocial Health on Adolescents and Young Adults with Gender Dysphoria Before and After Gender-Affirming Medical Interventions: A Descriptive Study from the Hamburg Gender Identity Service." *European Child & Adolescent Psychiatry* (September 2020). DOI.org /10.1007/s00787-020-01640-2.

Bränström, Richard, and John Pachankis. "Reduction in Mental Health Treatment Utilization Among Transgender Individuals after Gender-Affirming Surgeries: A Total Population Study." *European Journal of Public Health* 29, sup. 4 (November 2019). DOI.org/10.1093/eurpub/ckz185.465.

Cauldwell, David O. "Psychopathia Transexualis." *International Journal of Transgenderism* 5, no. 2 (2001). Retrieved from Web.Archive.org/web/20070610124058/http://www.sympo sion.com/ijt/cauldwell/cauldwell_02.htm, via The Wayback Machine.

Collin, Lindsay, Sari L. Reisner, Vin Tangpricha, and Michael Good- man. "Prevalence of Transgender Depends on the 'Case' Definition: A Systematic Review." *The Journal of Sexual Medicine* 13, no. 4 (April 2016): 613–626. DOI.org/10.1016 /j.jsxm.2016.02.001.

Dank, Meredith, Pamela Lachman, Janine M. Zweig, and Jennifer Yahner. "Dating Violence Experiences of Lesbian, Gay, Bisexual, and Transgender Youth." *Journal of Youth and Adolescence* 43, no. 5 (July 2013): 846–857. DOI.org/10.1007 /s10964-013-9975-8.

De Vries, Annelou L., Jenifer K. McGuire, Thomas Steensma, Eva Wagenaar, Theo A. H. Doreleijers, and Peggy Cohen-Kettenis. "Young Adult Psychological Outcome after Puberty Suppression and Gender Reassignment." *Pediatrics* 134, no. 4 (October 2014): 696–704. DOI.org/10.1542/peds.2013-2958.

Defreyne, Justine, Laurens D. Van de Bruaene, Ernst Rietzschel, Judith Van Schuylenbergh, and Guy T'Sjoen. "Effects of Gender-Affirming Hormones on Lipid, Metabolic, and Cardiac SURROGATE Blood Markers in Transgender Persons." *Clinical Chemistry* 65, no. 1 (January 2019): 119–134. DOI.org /10.1373/clinchem.2018.288241.

Diamond, Milton. "Transsexualism as an Intersex Condition." *Transsexualität in Theologie Und Neurowissenschaften* (2016): 43–54. DOI.org/10.1515/9783110434392-005.

Durwood, Lily, Katie McLaughlin, and Kristina Olson. "Mental Health and Self-Worth in Socially Transitioned Transgender Youth." *Journal of the American Academy of Child & Adolescent Psychiatry* 56, no. 2 (November 2016). DOI.org/10.1016 /j.jaac.2016.10.016.

European Society of Endocrinology. "Transgender Brains Are More Like Their Desired Gender from an Early Age," May 22, 2018. ESE-Hormones.org/media/1506/transgender-brains -are-more-like-their-desired-gender-from-an-early-age.pdf.

Giovanardi, Guido. "Buying Time or Arresting Development? The Dilemma of Administering Hormone Blockers in Trans Children and Adolescents." *Porto Biomedical Journal* 2, no. 5 (September 2017): 153–156. DOI.org/10.1016/j.pbj.2017.06.001.

Gottman, John, and Julie Gottman. *Level 1 Clinical Training Manual*. The Gottman Institute, 2016.

Greytak, Emily A., Joseph G. Kosciw, and Elizabeth Diaz. *Harsh Realities: The Experiences of Transgender Youth in Our Nation's Schools*. GLSEN, 2009. Retrieved from GLSEN.org /sites/default/files/2020-01/Harsh_Realities_The _Experiences_of_Transgender_Youth_2009.pdf.

Gruberg, S. "Beyond Bostock: The Future of LGBTQ Civil Rights." Center for American Progress, August 26, 2020. AmericanProgress.org/issues/lgbtq-rights/reports/2020 /08/26/489772/beyond-bostock-future-lgbtq-civil-rights.

Guillamon, Antonio, Carme Junque, and Esther Gómez-Gil. "A Review of the Status of Brain Structure Research in Transsexualism." *Archives of Sexual Behavior* 45, no. 7 (June 2016): 1615–1648. DOI.org/10.1007/s10508-016-0768-5.

Hale, Arthur E., Solana Y. Chertow, Yingjie Weng, Andrea Tabuenca, and Tandy Aye. "Perceptions of Support Among Transgender and Gender-Expansive Adolescents and Their Parents." *Journal of Adolescent Health* 68, no. 6 (June 2021): 1075–1081. DOI.org/10.1016/j.jadohealth.2020.11.021.

Hassouri, Paria. "What I Learned as a Parent of a Transgender Child." *The New York Times*, September 8, 2020. NYTimes.com /2020/09/08/well/family/transgender-child-parenting.html.

Heylens, Gunter, Charlotte Verroken, Sanne De Cock, Guy T'Sjoen, and Griet De Cuypere. "Effects of Different Steps in Gender Reassignment Therapy on Psychopathology: A Prospective Study of Persons with a Gender Identity Disorder." *The Journal of Sexual Medicine* 11, no. 1 (January 2014): 119–126. DOI.org/10.1111/jsm.12363.

James, Sandy, Jody Herman, Susan Rankin, Mara Keisling, Lisa Mottet, and Ma'ayan Anafi. *The Report of the 2015 U.S. Transgender Survey.* National Center for Transgender Equality, 2016. Retrieved from TransEquality.org/sites/default/files /docs/usts/USTS-Full-Report-Dec17.pdf.

Krafft-Ebing, Richard von. *Psychopathia Sexualis.* Philadelphia: F. A. Davis, 1893.

Nanda, Serena. "Hijra and Sadhin: Neither Man nor Woman in India." In *Gender Diversity: Crosscultural Variations.* Long Grove, IL: Waveland Press, 2014, 192–201.

National Institute on Drug Abuse. *How Does Anabolic Steroid Misuse Affect Behavior?* National Institute on Drug Abuse, 2021. Retrieved September 27, 2021, from DrugAbuse.gov /publications/research-reports/steroids-other-appearance -performance-enhancing-drugs-apeds/how-does-anabolic -steroid-misuse-affect-behavior.

Peitzmeier, Sarah, Ivy Gardner, Jamie Weinand, Alexandra Corbet, and Kimberlynn Acevedo. (2016). "Health Impact of Chest Binding Among Transgender Adults: A Community-Engaged, Cross-Sectional Study." *Culture, Health & Sexuality* 19, no. 1 (May 2016): 64–75. DOI.org/10.1080/13691058.201 6.1191675.

Savioni, Lucrezia, and Stefano Triberti. "Cognitive Biases in Chronic Illness and Their Impact on Patients' Commitment." *Frontiers in Psychology* 11 (October 2020). DOI.org/10.3389 /fpsyg.2020.579455.

Silk, Susan, and Barry Goldman. "How Not to Say the Wrong Thing." *Los Angeles Times*, April 7, 2013. LATimes.com/opinion /op-ed/la-xpm-2013-apr-07-la-oe-0407-silk-ring-theory -20130407-story.html.

Swartz, A. "'Are You Really Trans?': The Problem with Trans Brain Science." *IJFAB Blog*, October 14, 2018. IJFAB.org/blog /2018/07/3694.

Thomas, Wesley. "Navajo Cultural Constructions of Gender and Sexuality." In Sue-Ellen Jacobs, Wesley Thomas, and Sabine Lang (Eds.), *Two-Spirit People: Native American Gender Identity, Sexuality, and Spirituality*. Champaign, IL: University of Illinois Press, 2005.

Van de Grift, Tim C., Els Elaut, Susanne C. Cerwenka, Peggy Cohen-Kettenis, Griet De Cuypere, Hertha Richter-Appelt, and Bandewijntje Kreukels. "Effects of Medical Interventions on Gender Dysphoria and Body Image: A Follow-up Study." *Psychosomatic Medicine* 79, no. 7 (September 2017): 815–823. DOI.org/10.1097/psy.0000000000000465.

Varner, Eric. R. "Transcending Gender: Assimilation, Identity, and Roman Imperial Portraits." *Supplements to the Memoirs of the American Academy in Rome* 7 (2008): 185–205.

Weinand, Jamie D., and Joshua D. Safer. "Hormone Therapy in Transgender Adults Is Safe with Provider Supervision: A Review of Hormone Therapy Sequelae for Transgender Individuals." *Journal of Clinical & Translational Endocrinology* 2, no. 2 (June 2015): 55–60. DOI.org/10.1016/j.jcte .2015.02.003

What We Know Project. "What Does the Scholarly Research Say About the Effect of Gender Transition on Transgender Well-Being?" 2018. Retrieved from WhatWeKnow.Inequality .Cornell.edu/topics/lgbt-equality/what-does-the-scholarly -research-say-about-the-well-being-of-transgender -people.

Wiepjes, Chantal M., Nienke M. Nota, Christel de Blok, Maartje Klaver, Annelou de Vries, S. Annelijn Wensing-Kruger, Renate de Jongh, et al. "The Amsterdam Cohort of Gender Dysphoria Study (1972–2015): Trends in Prevalence, Treatment, and Regrets." *The Journal of Sexual Medicine* 15, no. 4 (February 2018): 582–590. DOI.org/10.1016/j.jsxm.2018.01.016.

Zweig, Janine M., Meredith Dank, Pamela Lachman, and Jennifer Yahner. *Technology, Teen Dating Violence and Abuse, and Bullying.* Urban Institute, Justice Policy Center, 2013. Retrieved from OJP.gov/pdffiles1/nij/grants/243296.pdf.

Index

Acknowledgments

I am grateful to my clients for everything they've taught me in more than a decade of practice, and for being patient with my mistakes. I credit my long-suffering partner, Sam Barbaro, for everything I've ever learned about how to be good to other people. Thanks also to my wonderful editor, Kayla Park, who shepherded this book from start to finish, and to this project's excellent development editor, Erika Sloan. And I owe many thanks to my dog, Broccoli, for teaching me how to clean pretty much any substance out of a shag carpet.

About the Author

 **Andrew Maxwell Triska, MSW, LCSW,** is a psychotherapist and author in New York who works with trans and queer youth and adults and specializes in anxiety, identity, and relationships. In addition to his clinical work and writing, Triska trains and consults on gender identity and sexuality for organizations, corporations, and schools. His other books include 2021's *Transgender Self-Care Journal* and *Gender Identity Workbook for Teens*. Triska is proud to be a trans-identified therapist.

CPSIA information can be obtained
at www.ICGtesting.com
Printed in the USA
JSHW051918120222
22810JS00004B/4

9 781638 788836